THE GOLDEN RULES
OF
ADVOCACY

THE GOLDEN RULES
OF
ADVOCACY

Keith Evans

OXFORD
UNIVERSITY PRESS

OXFORD
UNIVERSITY PRESS

Great Clarendon Street, Oxford OX2 6DP
Oxford University Press is a department of the University of Oxford.
It furthers the University's objective of excellence in research, scholarship,
and education by publishing worldwide in
Oxford New York
Auckland   Cape Town Dar es Salaam Hong Kong Karachi
Kuala Lumpur Madrid Melbourne Mexico City Nairobi
New Delhi Shanghai Taipei Toronto
With offices in
Argentina Austria Brazil Chile Czech Republic France Greece
Guatemala Hungary Italy Japan South Korea Poland Portugal
Singapore Switzerland Thailand Turkey Ukraine Vietnam

Oxford is a registered trade mark of Oxford University Press
in the UK and in certain other countries
Published in the United States
by Oxford University Press Inc., New York

ISBN 978-1-85431-259-4

Contents

for my learned friends
on the Western Circuit

for my attorney colleagues
at Gray, Cary, Ames & Frye
San Diego, California

and for Kit and Zoë

Introduction

Skilful advocacy is a rare commodity. Although every generation produces its small handful of great advocates and a variable crop of really competent ones, the bulk of lawyers out there, standing up in our courts, never perform as they should – and could.

It's been the same for centuries, all over the English-speaking world. It's because we don't operate a system that guarantees a lawyer will really know what he or she is doing before handling a trial. Qualify as a barrister, do a pupillage of one kind or another, and you have the immediate right to screw up somebody's case in court. Solicitors, albeit in a much narrower range of courts, don't even get the nominal training of a pupillage. We lawyers have been left with a huge field in which to demonstate our incompetence.

Certainly, there is advocacy training available and some of it is compulsory. There are courses you can take. But there still isn't a system in place which insists you *don't* go into court before you have shown that you *really* know what you are about.

Looked at from the point of view of the young advocate, we see the other, equally truthful, side of the coin. We are scared stiff of our first trials, always were. Our biggest fears are, one, that we are going to make fools of ourselves and, two, that we'll meet something we've never met before and we'll just not know what to do.

'Tell me, Mr Evans,' says the judge, interrupting my opening, 'is this a *Smith* v *Manchester* kind of case?'

'*Smith* v *Manchester*?' I ask myself, '*What* is a *Smith* v *Manchester* kind of case?'

It can be terrifying, and it usually takes years of practice to build your confidence as an advocate. During those years most of us learn mainly by trial and error. And that, when you think about it, means the *client's* trial and the *lawyer's* error.

One day, perhaps, things will be different. The time may come when we look back and wonder how we could have allowed our courts of law, the most important protectors of our freedoms, to be populated with under-trained advocates. And how we could have permitted to continue, all these centuries, the despairing disbelief of the client who suddenly realises his lawyer is hopeless.

Trial advocacy is a skill that can be taught. If the teacher is competent and if the student has the right frame of mind, and is willing to devote not more than 10 minutes a day to *thinking* about advocacy, then *anyone* capable of getting through the Bar finals or passing the solicitors' exams is also capable of becoming an excellent advocate. It is not a mystery: it is a skill.

Skills can be acquired.

This book will do more than get you started. If you devote two minutes a day to reading something in it, then another eight minutes thinking about what you have read, in two months you will already be better than 75 per cent of the competition out there. If you really interest yourself in it and take advocacy seriously, you'll almost certainly find yourself among the 10 per cent best advocates in the country. After that, native genius takes over and it's up to you.

By the time you come to the end of this book – and it's easy reading because it's the text of a live, one-day, seminar – you ought to find yourself feeling that good advocacy is mostly a matter of common sense. The trouble is that we lawyers often leave common sense behind when we go into court. As a result we often seem boring and pompous, and we make the stupidest mistakes again and again. We are so preoccupied with the complexities and the pressures of our position we forget all the common-sense simplicities. It's a barrier peculiar to the profession. Unless warned. almost all of us start out this way.

The Common Sense of Advocacy is what this book is about. It's organised into a series of Golden Rules, most of which should seem obvious when you've seen them, but not necessarily so obvious that you knew about them in advance. The Rules are illustrated clearly enough to demonstrate how they work, but the book does not contain more illustration than necessary. It is not a compendium of war stories, mine or anybody else's.

Get to know what these basic rules are, think about them and keep thinking about them, and you will avoid those miserable pitfalls that I fell into, along with most of my contemporaries.

If you are ready, let's get started.

THE DIMENSIONS

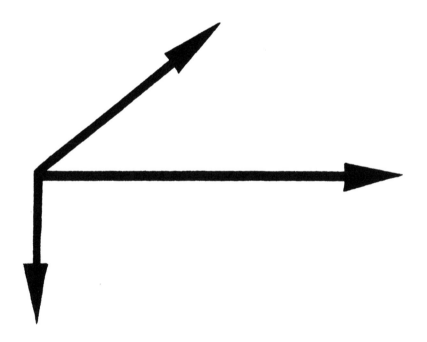

The Dimensions

We live in a three-dimensional world: up and down, sideways and to and fro. This is the hollow box in which human existence takes place. There are three fundamental truths which are so important to the advocate you can think of them as being the equivalent of the dimensions in which we live. All advocacy takes place in the context of these three truths. This is what they are.

FIRST DIMENSION

IN THE COMMON LAW COUNTRIES A TRIAL IS *NOT* AN EXERCISE DESIGNED TO DISCOVER THE TRUTH

Shocking though this idea may be at first, think about it. The factfinding tribunal – whether judge alone or jury – is not being asked to discover the truth about anything. Focus on just a handful of things you already know very well:

● The rules of evidence are mainly designed to exclude. They often operate to prevent the evidence actually presented from showing the truth of the matter at all.
● The jury rarely asks questions and if it does it is often told it can't have the answer.
● Personal knowledge of the dispute before the court can disqualify jurors.
● The judge is not an investigator but more like an umpire.
● The jury is not a committee of inquiry.

We could go on but we don't need to. Although it is hardly ever thought about and although it causes raised eyebrows even among lawyers, that rather shocking fact remains: we are *not* principally concerned with getting at the truth in the courtrooms of the English-speaking peoples. What we are doing as advocates is trying to get the factfinder to arrive at an *opinion*, an opinion in our favour. We are asking, in the case of a jury: 'On the admissible evidence presented in this trial – evidence which the judge has not told you to disregard, and in accordance with the appropriate burden and standard of proof – is it your *opinion* that this side succeeds or the other side?' In a trial by judge alone the principle is exactly the same.

This doesn't mean you have a licence to be dishonest. Anything but. You most certainly can't lie and you have to be desperately careful about concealing anything. The Bar Council can be quite Draconian in dealing with members who stray from its high standards of integrity. But, it's worth repeating, our objective at trial is *not* the ultimate truth but an opinion in our favour.

Remember this: by the time you get to trial, discovery is over. You should no longer be conducting an inquiry. Rather, *you should be putting on a presentation designed to persuade.* By realising this your whole attitude towards trial should change slightly. If you thought about it as a contest or a duel, start thinking about it more as a tightly controlled presentation.

SECOND DIMENSION

This is as different from the First Dimension as up and down is different from to and fro. It is this:

THE HUMAN ANIMAL IS
FAR MORE VIDEO THAN AUDIO

The way we collect most of our information is through our eyesight. Consider the use we make of our senses. In today's world touch is used mainly for enjoyment: we get a lot of information from handling things, but what a subsidiary sense this is. Smell is much the same for us humans, and so is taste: as devices by which we collect information, these first three senses take a back seat to sight and hearing. And when you compare sight and hearing you realise at once that the modern human being's principal means of fact gathering, of learning and of understanding, is eyesight.

We don't have a phrase 'hearing is believing'. We are used to television, video, cinema, newsprint, books. Listening is something we do with surprising rarity – intent listening, that is. Drive along with an educational tape in your player, a tape, for example, designed to bring you up to date on some legal topic. How many times have you found your mind wandering, have you realised that for several minutes you just haven't heard a thing? You nod off in your listening far, far more easily than in your seeing.

What we are asking judge or jury to do in court is to use their *second best device* for gathering understanding. And they do it: on the whole they do it well. But since we don't tie blindfolds on them they don't switch off their *best* information–gathering device. It is operating *all the time* while we are appealing to their second best device.

This obvious truth, this dimension of reality that we are operating in, has to be remembered at *all times*. People who have studied the psychology of communications have some terrifying statistics for us advocates. Examples:

- Sixty per cent of the message is conveyed by body language and visual appearance generally.
- Thirty per cent of the message is conveyed by tone of voice.
- Only 10 per cent of the message comes through the words used.
- Only 10 per cent of what people hear gets remembered. If, on the other hand, they see something connected with what they are hearing, as they are hearing it, they remember 50 per cent.

They didn't tell me these things before I qualified. I wasn't given this information during my pupillage. Lawyers tend not to know these statistics just as they don't seem to realise that they are operating virtually all the time in the Video Dimension.

Yet from the moment lawyers go into court the chances are they are going to be seen by one or more jurors. When they are in the courtroom itself they are under the scrutiny of the jury almost full time. This means that the advocate is conveying visual messages to judge and jury throughout the whole day. We just can't avoid it.

We *all* have body language. Without realising what we are signalling, we are in fact signalling something *all* the time. Since we can't help it, we simply must know what we are conveying. Appearances count more in the courtroom than most advocates are prepared to admit or think about. But we are public performers. No less than the actor, the fashion model and the politician we are making a visual impression all the time and we have a duty to our clients to know what that impression is.

Although we may be extremely embarrassed by the idea and no doubt painfully shy, we really ought to spend a regular session in front of a mirror, talking and moving and gesturing, simply to get to know ourselves and to *stay* knowing ourselves. If you can find the courage, try it tonight. Just discover for yourself how long you have to look at the most familiar face in the world before a complete stranger looks back at you. It takes a little less than two minutes with most people.

The adult human hardly ever gets a completely new and objective view of himself or herself, but we advocates have a duty to stay in touch with ourselves and know how we are coming across, visually, to the rest of the world. The video recorder is a wonderful tool for self-awareness. It's intimidating, but it will show you things you just hadn't been aware of: how you move your head, what you do with your mouth, your nose, your eyebrows and particularly your eyes. It will show you how you move your hands, your arms and your body generally. The lines on your forehead and around your nose are especially important. You can't know about any of these without making a study of yourself. This may seem terribly foreign to us, but it's of much greater importance than most of us are prepared to admit.

As soon as you do admit to yourself that yes, this Video Dimension is real, some common-sense rules are staring at you. The more you think about it the more you'll see, but the most obvious rules are as follows:

YOU MUST DRESS APPROPRIATELY

It has been said by one American judge that in her court the lawyer who wears polyester has the burden of proof. Jurors have surprisingly high expectations of lawyers and dress is important. The colours you wear, and that your client and witnesses wear, are much more significant than most of us ever pause to think about. If you've never encountered any of the studies that have been done on the impact of colour then make it your business to attend a seminar by an expert in the field. Until you have had it demonstrated to you, you are unlikely to appreciate what an astonishing effect the choice of appropriate and inappropriate colour can have on the impression made by the wearer.

Because we barristers still wear a uniform that dates back centuries, this doesn't mean that we are excused from the need to think about dress. The filthy, disintegrating wig and the shabby, torn gown may be a great statement of how you feel about tradition, but they ensure that you start at a disadvantage, and it's not fair to your client. Next:

DO NOT BE SEEN TO BE
IN TOO FRIENDLY A RELATIONSHIP
WITH YOUR OPPONENT

This is particularly important in courts where you know your opponents well. Even if you are the greatest of friends ouside the courtroom it is your duty when in the court building to conceal this. Plain courtesy is enough. The reason for this ought to be clear: if a juror or jurors should happen to see you, outside court, in an obviously friendly encounter with your opponent, and then see you, in court, in an adversarial situation with the same person, they are going to wonder about your sincerity. Is it all some sort of act in court? Some kind of game? If they see that you and your learned friend actually are on matey terms with each other they may well feel that the whole thing is an exercise in going through the motions. A trial is a serious affair, and anything which detracts from the jury's awareness of this is to be avoided.

DO NOT SMILE, LAUGH OR JOKE
WITHOUT INCLUDING THE JURY

Nothing is so off-putting and potentially alienating as seeing laughter and joking there in front of you without knowing what is going on and being able to share in the fun.

APPEAR AT ALL TIMES TO BE
ABSOLUTELY SINCERE

If you fail in this even one time you undermine your chances for the whole of the rest of the case.

NEVER CONVEY ANY VISUAL SIGNAL
YOU DO NOT INTEND TO CONVEY

This means you must never seem *surprised* unless you intend to, you must never seem *troubled* unless you intend to and you must never seem to be *expending effort* unless you intend to.

(And let me give you an encouraging hint. When you go to a new court, the only person who knows about your inexperience, nervousness and limitations is you yourself. To the rest of the world you may be an advocate of considerable experience and lethal talent. Don't throw away the advantage of their not knowing.)

Those rules all arise naturally out of the need to guard against the *dangers* of the Video Dimension. But it can be taken advantage of as well. Think how. It can be summarised in one obvious Golden Rule:

ENSURE THAT YOUR FACTFINDER ALWAYS
HAS SOMETHING TO LOOK AT

Since they are going to be using their eyes, provide them with a focus.

USE VISUAL AIDS

People *listen* far more intently if they have something to look at connected with what they are hearing, and they remember, according to the statistics, up to five times as much. Therefore, use a bundle of carefuly chosen exhibits, *clearly* drawn plans, photographs, enlargements of selected sentences or paragraphs. If you put such a bundle in front of your factfinder you *may* find it becomes the road-map that dictates the direction of the entire case.

The prosecution sometimes prepare excellent bundles: the defence often overlook the possibilities. Apart from anything else, if you have such a bundle, and use it properly, you'll find that you and your factfinder inevitably enter into a closer relationship with each other. 'Can we look at page 37, members of the jury?' gets them involved in doing something that *you* have initiated, and this almost invariably raises the energies flowing between you and them.

Try, if you possibly can, to get this bundle ready before the summons for directions, so that you can get the court to approve it in advance. This saves you from the need, at trial or just before, of tearing out pages that have been successfully objected to.

If you can get a video into court, get one. If you can get a model of some sort, get one of those too – particularly models that come apart. Get as many as you can. Give them something to look at.

Equally important,

MAINTAIN EYE CONTACT WITH THE FACTFINDER

Don't overdo it. The direct stare is usually seen as a threat in the animal kingdom and the human being is no exception. The regular glance is enough, resting on your factfinder's eyes long enough not to seem shifty, and briefly enough not to seem threatening or intrusive. You not only stay in touch this way: you usually get a lot of feedback, feedback from which you can gauge how you are doing.

I'll never forget an incident that happened at Snaresbrook, many years ago. My opponent, incredibly, never looked at the jury once during a week-long trial. Whenever he faced in their direction he either had his eyes fixed on his notes or rolled back in his head, so that all one could see was the whites of his eyes. It was quite fascinating and the jury were visibly puzzled all the way through.

If the time should ever come when you are asked to sit as a judge – and England and Wales rely heavily on their recorders, deputies and assistants of all kinds – you will be astonished at how much you can see. Counsel, *and* their solicitors' representatives, frequently signal how their case is going and thus *draw attention* to things that might otherwise have gone unnoticed. Take care.

Enough then about the Video Dimension. When you've seen how important it is you can start to work out for yourself how to guard against it and take advantage of it. Be creative.

The last of the three dimensions is as different from the first two as they were from each other. Come now to the next absolutely fundamental truth.

THIRD DIMENSION

PEOPLE DO NOT LIKE LAWYERS!

We lawyers have been near the bottom of the popularity polls for centuries, keeping company with executioners, horse-traders and debt-collectors. It's not as bad in England as it is in America, but the respect which used to be accorded to the barrister, in his imposing antique uniform, is nothing like as great as it used to be. The public still think of us as making vast sums of money, but they are much less forelock-tugging than in the past, and some of them are hypercritical of the entire legal profession. Look at some of the things thoughtful people have said about lawyers. Come back to the 14th century, at the time of the Peasants' Revolt. The first place the mob made for was the Inns of Court. They burned them down. A contemporary account:

> It was marvellous to see how the most aged and infirm of them scrambled off with the agility of rats or evil spirits!

Or how about the 18th century, at a time before the title of 'solicitor' was in general use? Dr Sam Johnson:

> I don't care to speak ill of anyone behind his back, but I do believe that gentleman is an attorney.

Or the 19th century – Sir John Simon:

> The public see the lawyer as an unprincipled wretch who is constantly engaged in the distortion of the truth by methods entirely discreditable and for rewards grossly exaggerated. He is expected to be a hypocrite.

The 19th century again – Jeremy Bentham:

> The parties pay their way through the offices of the High Court like
> half-starved flies crawling through a row of spiders.

Or the bill sent by an English solicitor:

> To crossing the Strand to discuss your case with you: six and
> eightpence. To recrossing the Strand when I discovered it wasn't
> you: six and eightpence.

One could make an entire book out of the anti-lawyer jokes in the
20th century. We are a heartily disliked profession. People are afraid
of us. In many ways they *despise* us. 'Ignorance of the law doesn't
prevent the losing attorney from collecting his fee.'

So what Golden Rules arise out of this sorry but quite fundamental
truth? How do we work against this prejudice? Let me give you just
three.

STICK RIGOROUSLY TO THE TRUTH

There actually is a way in which every case can be conducted with
absolutely total honesty. There is no need at all for an advocate to be
two-faced. Search for the way in which you can present your case in
total sincerity. Quite apart from anything else, the composite mind
that a jury becomes has an incredible nose for insincerity. If you don't
believe what you are asking them to believe then make no mistake
about it: *they will know.*

Too many advocates don't realise this. If you can't find a way of doing
a case with utmost sincerity then settle or plead, or get someone else
to do it. But it doesn't have to come to that. There is a sincere way of
conducting every case. Find it.

Imagine, for example, a criminal case. You are defending someone in
the teeth of really difficult evidence. His story just isn't credible. You
dare not put him in the witness-box. What do you do? You have to
have recourse to the burden of proof. You hammer home the
importance that no one be convicted unless the offence is proved

beyond reasonable doubt. You tell them what reasonable doubt is all about; you tell the jury that unless they have been corralled by the prosecution evidence, unless they have been pushed into a corner by it so that they are left with no sensible choice in the matter, then they *must* come in with a not guilty verdict. Paint the picture for them of what a messy failure a miscarriage of justice is. Tell them about the way it has happened in the past. Put the fear of God into them over what would happen to individual safety if we didn't take the burden of proof as seriously as we do. If your client gets convicted after that, he's almost certainly guilty. There is always a totally honest way of presenting a case. Find it and do it that way.

DON'T APPEAR TO BE MANIPULATIVE

We all know when we are being manipulated. If it's your five-year-old daughter who's doing it it can be charming. In most other situations it's offensive. If you make the jury feel that you are manipulating them they'll feel that you are living down to their expectations and they'll mistrust you for it. Take care, too, not to come across as a manipulator of witnesses.

DON'T SOUND LIKE A LAWYER

This isn't easy, particularly for a member of the Bar. We spent all those years learning a whole new vocabulary as well as a whole new way of thinking. It's our vocabulary: we like it: it's useful.

'Serjeant Sullivan,' said the president of the Court of Appeal, 'hasn't your client ever heard of *in pari delicto potior est conditio defendentis?*'

'My Lord,' replied the great Irish advocate, 'in the hills and dales of Killarney where my client plies his trade as a shepherd, they talk of little else!'

Don't use it! When you are in front of a jury don't use any more lawyer's language than you absolutely have to. People don't control motor vehicles, they drive cars. They don't enter into contractual arrangements. They don't partake of alcoholic beverages. 'At the end of the day' is when ordinary people leave their place of work or go to bed. If you use that phrase to mean 'when everything is borne in mind', you are going to sound like a lawyer and they may very well not understand what you are talking about.

Play a game with yourself during all those long waits that afflict our profession: see how long a list you can make of lawyers' words we could perfectly well do without. Examine your language from this day on. Strip out *anything* that sounds lawyerish. Find some other way of saying what you want to say. Work hard at it because it really matters. The Golden Rule is clear: *Do not sound like a lawyer any more than is absolutely necessary.*

Those, then, are the three fundamental truths, the three Dimensions in the context of which all courtroom advocacy takes place. But in real life there is an extra, a Fourth Dimension, and it is very much there in court as well.

FOURTH DIMENSION

TIME

Time. Your time. My time. If you are any good at what you do it's expensive, valuable stuff. Some of you measure your profitability by time. Time to the lawyer can be enemy or paymaster. Time is a demanding mistress, a jealous lover, a gaoler, a slave-driver.

It can also be elastic. Compare 10 minutes making love with 10 minutes in the dentist's chair having a filling done. And think of how long-drawn-out five hours in a jury-box listening to an incompetent, wasteful advocate can be. Most jurors have better things to do with their time. We don't pay them very much, and they are giving their time as a public duty. They have to rush around outside court hours getting everything done just so they can sit there and listen to you, *you*, hour after hour, day after day, perhaps even week after week.

And what about the judge? Do you know how much is usually waiting to be done, on the other side of the corridor? Do you know how much paper has to be looked at just to stay abreast of the workload?

This is the Fourth Dimension in which you operate as an advocate, and if you forget it, if you forget it for one moment of your factfinder's precious time, look out! If you *ever* give them cause to feel that you are wasting their time they will resent you for it, and if you get your factfinder feeling resentful about you, you are a good halfway to losing your case. This is far, far more important than most lawyers realise.

It's worse than that. It's not just that the inexperienced advocate hasn't grasped the problems of the Fourth Dimension. There is an opposite pressure that works on us and we usually give way before it. It's a two-pronged thing.

First prong. You've got a client. The client is almost certainly in court, listening intently to everything. You feel this huge obligation to make sure she feels she is being properly represented. You have this conviction that you ought to be giving her so many questions in cross-examination, so many square feet of transcript. If you don't do this, isn't she going to feel that you didn't do your best for her, that you sold her short, that you let her down?

She may indeed. And she would be as wrong as you were. This is something you must talk to her about in advance. This is part of the *private advocacy* that goes on between counsel and client. You've got to explain it, make her understand the Fourth Dimension, make her appreciate that brevity is your secret weapon. When she sees the quality of attention you are getting from your factfinder she'll stop worrying about it, but, yes, you do have a duty to explain all this to your client in advance.

Second prong. The other kind of pressure that will push you into wasting time is your own insecurity. You'll be convinced that you didn't make yourself clear enough, didn't say it forcefully enough, didn't get your point across adequately. And you will repeat yourself. It's so understandable, this fear, this anxiety. We've all suffered from it and know the pressure.

Don't yield to it.

DON'T REPEAT YOURSELF

Take your courage in both hands, say it once as clearly as you can
and *don't say it twice*. The exceptions to this are very few and we'll
come to them later.

Now, one last point before we move on. Can you take advantage of
the Dimension of Time? We saw that the Video Dimension had
advantages as well as dangers, and we thought through how to tap in
to those advantages. Can we do the same with Time? Certainly we
can, and it's easy.

All you have to do is remember, now and again, to drop in a phrase
to remind everybody that Time is something you are aware of.

'I want to deal with this as briefly as I can, Mr Witness.'

'Well, I don't want to take up any more time on that point. Let's
move on.'

'Well, let me move quickly to something else. I want to ask you
about . . .'

You don't have to use these particular phrases. Anything along these
lines will do. Just make sure that you get across to your judge, or
judge and jury, every day, preferably twice a day, that you know the
importance of Time. Their Time. You will warm their hearts.

THE MANDATORY RULES

The Mandatory Rules

Before we get down to looking at the Golden Rules that apply to all advocacy, let's spend a little while on a small handful of rules that should be thought of as mandatory. These really *must* be observed. If you break them you'll show yourself to be unprofessional. Some of them are so important that breaking them can lead to a retrial. Since the Mandatory Rules are so few there is no excuse for not knowing them. What are they?

MANDATORY RULE NUMBER ONE

THE ADVOCATE MUST NOT EXPRESS HIS OR HER OPINION IN COURT

This is one of those Rules that pupillage teaches fairly successfully and which is broken all the time in America, but it's well worth a moment to reinforce it. Let's consider some basic ideas. First, an advocate doing a trial is a licensed professional. You are there to represent only one side of the dispute – a kind of hired champion. Think of what the job involves. What are its limits? You are there to present and test the evidence as effectively as possible, to present and argue the relevant law when you deal with submissions or objections, then to sum up the whole lot as attractively as you can. That's it. Your opinion about the merits of the case doesn't enter into that process, anywhere at all. Let me digress for a moment.

The cab rank rule is being talked about quite a lot these days, and threatens to be used in ways that would have appalled our predecessors. It had nothing at all to do with money and payment when it was first adopted. It came into existence to avoid unpopular defendants finding themselves at trial with no one to represent them, and it says this: if you are offered a case that is within your field of expertise, then, if the client is willing to pay what you usually charge and your diary shows you are free to take the case, you don't have any choice in the matter: you *must* accept it. If you turn it down you can be disciplined, even disbarred! It's your duty to take it and do your best for the client. It's absolutely irrelevant whether you think you are doing a winner or a loser.

Because of this rule, no one in court is ever going to embarrass you by asking what you actually think about the merits of your case. Some years ago a judge was trying a difficult patent dispute. Counsel on both sides were nationally recognised experts in their field. The judge was having a devil of a time grappling with the problem and at one stage he threw down his pen in despair and looked at the lawyer addressing him. 'Oh, Mr S——,' he said, 'how I wish I could ask you what you really think about this case!' But he couldn't. Counsel is there to urge one side of the dispute. You are *not* allowed to express an opinion.

Another short illustration. The American revolutionary, Tom Paine, was put on trial in England on a political charge. He was defended by the leading barrister of the day, Thomas Erskine. The trial was about the liberty of the individual, and although it isn't much remembered today there was actually a huge amount of support in England for the colonists. At one point Erskine, in a towering passion, said to the judge, 'And now, my Lord, I will lay aside the role of advocate and address you as a man!' Lord Campbell, the judge trying the case, broke in on him at once. 'You will do nothing of the sort!' he said. 'The only right and licence you have to appear in this court is as an advocate!' And the judge was absolutely right.

But the rule is broken all the time in America. 'It is our opinion, ladies and gentlemen, that when you have heard the evidence, you'll have no difficulty in returning a verdict for the plaintiff.' 'I think, ladies and gentlemen, you will find the evidence of Mr Fagin credible and satisfactory.' 'We feel that you'll be left in no doubt etc. etc.' Happily, the English advocate doesn't offend nearly so much. It's none of your business to tell the factfinder what you think of the merits. There is a real risk the jury will feel you are trespassing on their ground; but the real harm lies in the effect it has on your judge. Break this rule and it marks you off as unprofessional. It is the clearest signal that you have never heard of the rule, that you don't know your job properly. It makes your judge suspicious of you, makes him wonder what else you are going to do wrong, how much you can't be trusted. And if he feels this you can be sure he'll be more ready to rule against you when the other side objects to something. You have tipped the balance of the judge's inclination in your opponent's favour.

So how do you cope? How do you manage to sound sincere without breaching this rule and branding yourself as unprofessional? It's very easy. You just avoid using the words 'I think' or 'I believe' or 'it's my opinion' when you are talking about anything to do with the merits of the case. Instead of saying 'I believe you will be convinced that . . .', you say, 'I trust that, when you have heard what the witnesses have to tell you, you will be convinced that . . .'. Instead of 'we feel' you say 'we hope'. You say it in a low, throw-away tone of voice, emphasising the meat of the sentence that follows. You lose nothing at all in sincerity and impact, but you send a minor signal straight to your judge that you are one advocate, at any rate, who knows the No Opinion Rule. And getting that message to your judge, that you know what you are doing, and getting it across as early in the trial as possible, is vital.

I've taken time to explain this fully because it's so important. The rest of the Mandatory Rules we can deal with much more quickly. The next one should be obvious, but since I've often seen it broken let me spell it out.

MANDATORY RULE NUMBER TWO

AS AN ADVOCATE YOU NEVER GIVE EVIDENCE YOURSELF – OR APPEAR TO GIVE EVIDENCE

Let me give an illustration of the kind of thing I mean. I had a pupil about 18 years ago, who happened to get briefed in a case I was doing. I represented one defendant: he represented the other. It was a

criminal matter in front of a jury. He did it beautifully. He
cross-examined skilfully although he was trembling like a leaf. He
argued points of admissibility like an expert. I was proud of him and
I was looking forward to see how he'd do in his final speech. He did
that beautifully too, but all of a sudden I heard him say: 'And, do you
know, members of the jury, I was talking to my client over the lunch
hour and he told me . . .!'. Up went the judge's eyebrows. Up jumped
our opponent, spluttering an objection. I grabbed my pupil's gown
and hissed in his ear. He turned quickly to something else, but later,
when the jury had gone out he came to me, really bewildered.

'What did I do wrong?'

I explained.

'You never told me that before,' he said reproachfully. And I realised
that what was obvious to me may not be obvious to everyone else.
And it's not in the books. That's why I include this in the Mandatory
Rules. Evidence comes from the witness-box, never from the
advocate. That trial, incidentally, had a nice ending for my pupil. His
client was acquitted and mine was found guilty. That little war story
illustrates the next Mandatory Rule as well.

MANDATORY RULE NUMBER THREE

IN YOUR FINAL SPEECH SPEAK ONLY
OF THINGS WHICH HAVE BEEN TOUCHED UPON
IN THE EVIDENCE

How strictly must it be observed? Aren't there any generalities I can
talk about so as to spice up my closing remarks? If, in an
environmental case, I want to talk about the ecological dangers that
the planet is facing, or, in a drug case, the way the authorities seem
to be losing in the war against the traffickers, can't I do this? Does it
all have to be 'touched on' during the evidence stage before I can refer
to any generalities at all?

No, of course not. You can always talk about things that really are
common knowledge. You can always refer to verses from the Bible,

quotes from Shakespeare and Mark Twain. You don't have to prove by evidence where Birmingham is located. If, on the other hand, you needed to refer to the exact mileage between Birmingham's city centre and Charing Cross, that's something you should have raised during the evidence phase. You could probably have got the judge to take judicial notice of the distance and avoid having to call a witness, but you cannot refer to details like that without some kind of proof. The dividing line is almost always obvious. If you know the Mandatory Rule it should cause you no difficulty. Apart from that which is really common knowledge, speak only of things which have been touched on in the evidence.

MANDATORY RULE NUMBER FOUR

MAKE ABSOLUTELY SURE YOU 'PUT YOUR CASE' TO OPPOSING WITNESSES

This is an English rule which astonishes American lawyers and which is responsible, in large part, for the 'idiom' of English advocacy. You are supposed to know exactly what your client and your own witnesses are going to say when you call them, and if this is different from what the opposing witnesses say, then you have to 'put' your version to those witnesses when you come to cross-examine them. It's a strange rule in some ways. Members of the Bar are not allowed to talk to witnesses beforehand and we have to gather what they are likely to say from the 'proof of evidence' that may or may not be adequately prepared by instructing solicitors. Yet if we fail to 'put' our side's version to opposing witnesses we will be severely criticised by the judge and probably by our opponent as well. If you don't 'put' your case in cross-examination, and thus give the opposing witness the chance to deal with *your* version of what happened, it will be *presumed* against *your* witnesses, when they come out with something you failed to 'put', that they are making it up as they go along – perjuring themselves, in fact.

The requirement of this Mandatory Rule can lead you into sounding very much like a lawyer. 'I put it to you that . . .' is one of our ultimate pompous-sounding phrases. So it's worth bearing in mind that you don't have to use those actual words. As long as you give opposing

witnesses a fair chance to deal with your version of events you are
doing what the rule requires. So, 'Isn't this what happened, Mr
Snooks? You took a suitably coloured pen and altered just those few
figures on the account sheet?' is a perfectly fair way of doing it.

This rule can also lead you into the danger of appearing to argue with
the witness. Be terribly careful about this. When putting your case,
be quietly firm, show no surprise at the denials you attract and be as
brief as you can be.

MANDATORY RULE NUMBER FIVE

NEVER REFER TO THE CRIMINAL RECORD OF AN ACCUSED PERSON OR TO ANY OFFERS OF SETTLEMENT

If you do you'll have to start the trial all over again. In the rarest, the
very rarest, of circumstances there may be exceptions to this rule. In
a cut-throat criminal defence between several accused being tried
together it may be permissible for one to refer to the criminal record
of another. In very rare cases the prosecutor may be entitled to prove
the accused's previous convictions – as, for example, in firearms
cases. But situations like this involve the law of evidence and criminal
procedure, and no advocate worth the name would break this rule
without doing the most careful research *and* getting the prior
approval of the judge.

Likewise, it is conceivable that a case might occur when an offer of
settlement became relevant to the trial itself. Again it would be a
matter of scrupulously careful research *and* prior approval from the
judge before you breathe a word about it in court.

Waiting for my case to be called on in the Uxbridge County Court
once, I saw a splendid young fellow, obviously a few years my senior,
rise to his feet. Nonchalantly he explained to the judge how he had
taken over the next case from other counsel who had made a gaffe.

'Unfortunately, your Honour,' he chuckled, 'my predecessor was
foolish enough to tell the learned judge that there had been a payment
in of £750, and of course the matter had to go before another judge.'

'I see', said his Honour, 'Where would you like to go from here?'

MANDATORY RULE NUMBER SIX

NEVER PUT WORDS INTO THE MOUTH
OF YOUR OWN WITNESS

Another way of stating this rule is to say: don't ask any leading questions of your own witnesses. But if you think of it as not putting words into their mouths you sidestep the confusion that can sometimes arise over what is or what is not a leading question. Let's deal with this now, get it clear once and for all, then move on to the more entertaining Golden Rules. What exactly is a leading question? It's a question that contains its own answer: it's a question that can be answered with a Yes or a No, with a nod or a shake of the head.

'You are now 27 years old?' 'Mm.'
'You were born in Bridgend, South Wales?' 'Mm.'
'You fought in the Falklands, is that right?' 'Mm.'
'And you were wounded there?' 'Mm.'

Every question contains its own answer. All the witness has to do is agree.

If we change those questions so as to eliminate the answers they contain, they become:

'How old are you?'
'Twenty-seven.'
'Where were you born?'
'Bridgend, South Wales.'
'Did you play any part in the Falklands?'
'I was in the fighting.'
'How did you fare, personally?'
'I was wounded.'

Just because a question can be answered with a nod or a shake of the head it doesn't follow that it's leading. But the other way around, the rule is firm. A leading question can always be answered by a grunt, a nod, a shake of the head. A leading question always gives the witness the chance of adopting or rejecting the information it already contains.

So what is so bad about leading questions? Why do the rules say you can't use them on your own witnesses? Because with leading questions the evidence is coming not from the witness but from the advocate. It offends against Mandatory Rule Number Two – no evidence from the advocate – but it is offensive for two other very good reasons:

First, if the evidence comes from you and is merely adopted by your witness, how can the factfinders assess the witness's credibility? If all they hear is a series of yes or no answers they have nothing to go on. Your witness might have been someone you hired from a temp agency just to come to court to say yes or no at the appropriate places.

Second, if *you* give the evidence by putting words into your witness's mouth, you are ruining its value. You are diluting its effect to the point where it may be virtually useless. American jurors interviewed at the end of trials (where this is not only permitted but actively encouraged by the judge) have been asked about this and they are surprisingly clear in what they say. They easily recognise that evidence obtained by leading questions is pretty worthless. It is obvious to them that the witness was simply saying what the lawyer wanted her to say. And this reminds them, subconsciously – and sometimes consciously – of the Third Dimension: People don't like lawyers. People don't trust us. You let the jury feel your witness is only saying what you want her to say and you not only diminish the value of her evidence, you kindle the resentment of the jury. You lose both ways. So it's not only a Mandatory Rule that you don't put words into your own witness's mouth: it's an obvious Golden Rule of Advocacy as well. Although there are exceptions and although there are many instances where you can use leading questions on your own witnesses, be aware of the dangers. Even when you are allowed to, use them with utmost care.

So much, then, for the Mandatory Rules. Now let's take a trip to the theatre.

ADVOCACY AS THEATRE

Advocacy as Theatre

Listen to the following fragment of conversation:

'What was your jury service like?'
'It was great. Better than watching television.'
'But wasn't it boring?'
'Boring? Not at all! It was like being at the theatre all the way through.'
'But wasn't it difficult, coming to a decision?'
'Absolutely not. By the time we had to reach a verdict it was a foregone conclusion.'
'Would you want to do it again?'
'Definitely!'

Is this a fictitious conversation? Oh no. That is what your juror should be telling his friends after a trial which *you* conducted. I've said it already and I'll break one of my own rules by repeating myself. You are a licensed professional. The court of law is theatre. It should be professional theatre. Your job is to *make* it professional theatre – not amateur dramatics. Think about it.

You wouldn't want to be an advocate if there weren't something of an actor inside you. You'd have gone for another area of law practice, perhaps even another job altogether. By aiming for the courtroom you have chosen to go on the professional stage, just as surely as if you'd tried to make it in the West End or on television. Admit this to yourself. There's part of you that's stage-struck. If there isn't, get out now, because those of us who *are* stage-struck and honestly admit it are going to have a terrific advantage over you. If you can't reach into yourself and find the actor, move over to some other kind of lawyering, draw leases, draft contracts. You'll be safer back in an office where you don't have to put yourself on the line every time you stand up and open your mouth, where you don't have to take your courage in both hands and risk screwing up in public every time you go to court.

Advocacy is the sharp end of the law: it's where the real action is. As an advocate you've got to know how to handle fright – fear that rarely goes away completely – and handle it so no one would ever guess. To be a real advocate you've *got* to be an actor and you've got to be a brave one.

This needs to be said, you know. It needs to be faced. It's the basic, rock-bottom truth of what real advocacy is all about. It's the most demanding kind of lawyering there is. It takes courage, it takes imagination, and it takes the ability to get up and keep going when your mouth goes dry and you want to burst into tears. And all without showing it – all, incidentally, without letting it break your heart and break your spirit.

If you are going to be an advocate, here is your most important Golden Rule:

COMMIT TO IT. DON'T DO ANYTHING BY HALVES.
IF YOU CAN'T DEDICATE YOURSELF TO IT,
MOVE OVER AND DO SOMETHING ELSE

You've all got degrees: you all passed the exams. By definition you are among the most intelligent people in society. If you really and truly dedicate yourself to becoming a first-class advocate it is almost certain you will succeed. If you don't do this you will never be better than second-rate. All the other Golden Rules of Advocacy are subordinate to this one.

When I was head of chambers I tried to meet as many as I could of the young people who applied to us for a tenancy or for pupillage. It sometimes proved a disheartening experience. A lot of them were coming to the bar for ill-defined reasons, and they had virtually no acquaintance with any of the great writings about advocates and advocacy. Far from trying to immerse themselves in the subject, they had made no real inquiry into what it was about. Many had never had the curiosity even to go to court and watch a trial. It didn't augur well, either for them or for the future of advocacy in England. Many of them are out there in the courts now, and neither they nor others like them offer much competition to the young advocate who takes the calling seriously.

Amateurism is still much admired by the British. We have a liking for nonchalance and the appearance of effortless superiority, and getting too enthusiastic about anything is still felt to be a little ungentleman-ly. Where these facets of our national character came from in the first place hardly matters – they may have had something to do with centuries of enmity between us and the allegedly excitable French – but what does matter is that we still retain a cultural, perhaps even innate, respect for the amateur. This exposes us to a serious risk. Underneath the surface of apparent effortlessness there is usually an enormous amount of focused and dedicated hard work, but because this doesn't show it is easy for the onlooker to mistake nonchalance of performance for nonchalance of preparation.

Do try to avoid this pitfall. Take your advocacy seriously. Search out and read everything you can on the subject. Some of what you'll find you can skim. Some of it will be wonderfully entertaining as well as instructive.

If I'm beginning to sound like a revivalist preacher, forgive me. The British people are facing some pretty daunting challenges at the moment. Change and instability are going to be a fact of life for the foreseeable future, and this is very likely to tempt governments into as much authoritarianism as they can get away with. The skilled, courageous advocate is going to be needed as never before if what remains of our liberty isn't going to disappear. Real dedication is called for, real commitment to doing the job as well as it can possibly be done.

And if commitment to advocacy generally is important, so is dedication to the individual case. I know the system here doesn't always provide the opportunity for intensive preparation: it can sometimes be a matter, quite literally, of reading the papers on your way to court. But this isn't always the case, and even if you get thrown the papers the night before with miserable regularity, fight hard against the temptation to wing it. When you do get the chance for intensive preparation, take the opportunity.

Do it, and the rewards are guaranteed. You may not win your case, but you will impress your judge and jury from first to last. Nothing comes across more clearly. Obvious preparation, leading to a meticulous knowledge of the case, shines all the way through and *always* commands respect. Judges, asked what the single most important thing is about advocacy, say, again and again, '*Preparation!*' It's the best investment of them all. There's no substitute for it, and lack of preparation is always found out.

Let me bring you back to the concept of the courtroom as theatre.

Focus on this and a handful of Golden Rules leap out at you. Let's look at what they are. Let's examine some obvious buzz-words. What should theatre be? What does it involve?

Entertainment. Drama. A good story-line. Profound attentiveness from the audience. Applause. A sense that the whole thing was worthwhile doing, worthwhile having gone to. Good theatre is satisfying, moving, memorable. In good theatre, time never drags, the development of the play never flags, the audience never gets bored.

That's enough. There are more than enough ideas there to get started with. Let's take these out of the theatre and across to the courtroom and see how our Golden Rules emerge.

One thing is blindingly obvious, isn't it? In the lawcourt your audience can't get up and leave. They are in the truest sense captive. They aren't free to hiss and boo you off the stage. They are obliged to sit there, and this means that two things have to be borne in mind:

First: although they are obliged to sit there, *they are not obliged to listen to you.*

Second: since you have a captive audience you *must* regard yourself as obliged to make it as entertaining for them as you possibly can.

If you do make it entertaining they will unquestionably listen to you. If you don't they almost certainly won't. What listening they do will be done out of a sense of duty: it won't be intent listening and it won't be sympathetic to you or your case.

So, as an obvious, practical Golden Rule of Advocacy we have:

ENTERTAIN THEM

Simple as that.

But hold on, you say. Certainly it's an obvious Golden Rule. But you can't say, as you just did, 'Simple as that!' Stating the Rule and putting it into operation are very different things. Aren't they?

Well, no, not really. I'll suggest a handful of easy-to-use *tools* for keeping your factfinder entertained, and I'll come to them in a moment. But first I want to emphasise something. Just as there is a magical element about the theatre and acting, so there is a magical element about the court and advocacy, and part of that magic is this: if you are simply *aware* of a rule and only *hope* you'll be able to put it into operation, you are very unlikely to offend against it.

Take comfort from this because it's true. Simply by wanting to put the rules into effect you *will* put them into effect. You may not do it terribly well but you'll do it. Unless you are cursed with a total lack of imagination – and the chances of that are very small – then merely by knowing what the rules are and thinking about them as you prepare for trial, you will almost certainly not break them. And this, as I said at the outset, will put you ahead of most of the competition. Many of them don't seem to know there *are* any rules.

But I said I had some easy-to-use tools for keeping your factfinder entertained. Let's look at these. They are such basic, important, techniques that they can be thought of as Golden Rules in their own right. *First,*

TELL THEM A STORY

Keep this idea in the forefront of your mind all the way through, from the beginning of your preparation to the end of the case. Bear it in mind from your opening right through to your final speech. No matter what you are doing, what stage of the case you are at, always keep asking yourself whether there is an element of story-telling in what you are giving them.

Why do I recommend this? Because no one can resist listening to a well-told story, even if they've heard it before. This is how we human beings are. This is how we responded as children, listening with deep contentment to the same stories again and again. We never lose our capacity to respond. If we *feel* we are being told a story, if we sense that there is a story here, then our natural, instinctive, response is to prick up our ears and let it flow into us. An example:

> 'Ladies and gentlemen, let me tell you what I expect the evidence to prove in this case you've sworn to try. It actually was a dark and stormy evening. Winter was coming on and the road across the Dales was wet and slippery. Squalls were bringing sudden heavy showers of rain. Driving along that road in a little blue car were Jane and Richard Roe. They had been married for about two weeks. Jane was a primary school teacher: Richard had just completed his residency at a London hospital and was now a fully qualified doctor. They were both keen tennis players. Jane was a county champion in gymnastics. Because of the intermittent rain and the condition of the road they were going carefully, rarely travelling faster than 40 mph. It was Richard who was at the wheel.'

Do you want to know what happened next? Can you feel the mounting sense of doom? Are you wondering what on earth happened to these two nice young people?

Some of what you do in court will literally be a story: your opening will be, certainly. But you should aim, with every witness you call, to turn the evidence into a story as well. Even your cross-examinations can have the flavour of storytelling if you do it right. *Think* storytelling. If you do, you are likely to call into play your factfinder's natural impulse to listen. Surprisingly, this even applies, albeit to a lesser extent, to trial by judge alone.

Next, and very connected with the storytelling rule:

THINK BEGINNING, MIDDLE AND END

If you do you will automatically bring a shape to everything you do, whether it's an opening statement or a cross-examination. In particular, try to focus on how you intend to *end* whatever it is you are doing. This ensures, again almost automatically, that you always know where you are going. One of the rules we will come to when we deal with the examination of witnesses is the 'Always Know Your Objective Rule'. If you make a habit of thinking Beginning, Middle and End, with particular emphasis on End, you'll find that the Know Your Objective Rule almost takes care of itself.

The next tool in holding their attention and keeping them entertained is this:

MAINTAIN YOUR CONTINUITY

When you have a pause, when indeed a pause is forced upon you because your mind goes blank – as happens to all of us – try to make even that pause part of the entertainment. It can be done, and it's not difficult. Let me share with you a technique I was taught years ago by a very senior member of the Bar.

We all know the fright of having our minds go blank on us. For the inexperienced advocate it's a real fear. But it needn't be. What the technique involves is this, and it works in three stages.

When you suddenly realise, with alarm, that your mind has gone blank:

Step one is to send a message to your stomach and command it to relax. This actually does control the flow of adrenalin, and, with it, the dry mouth and the raised heartbeat.

Step two is to pick up any piece of paper with writing, type or printing on it, look intently at a blank margin, and silently count to three.

Step three is to glance up at your judge and say, 'If your Lordship would give me a moment', then look *straight* back at your piece of paper.

You can have 10 seconds at that point, 20 seconds of total silence, if you need them, to gather your thoughts. Nobody is going to mind. Nobody is going to feel that you have interrupted the continuity or that you have a breakdown in transmission. This is because *you have invested that pause with an apparent significance of its own.* You won't need 20 seconds. Your mind will clear much quicker than that, and on you go.

The next Golden Rule for holding their attention and keeping them entertained:

KEEP IT SIMPLE

Consider just one sentence from George Washington's first inaugural address, 30 April 1789:

> All I dare hope is that if, in executing this task, I have been too much swayed by a grateful remembrance of former instances, or by an affectionate sensibility to this transcendent proof of the confidence of my fellow citizens, and have thence too little consulted my incapacity as well as disinclination for the weighty and untried cases before me, my error will be palliated by the motives which mislead me, and its consequences be judged by my country with some share of the partiality in which they originated.

Most people, today, are lost by halfway through the second line. If you are forced to read on, or listen on, the chances are you'll become as dazed as if you had been hit over the head with a blunt instrument. Times have changed, and, for better or for worse, language has changed as well.

We human beings are largely what we have been conditioned to be. After 40 years of television people have come to expect sentences to be short. A sound bite of longer than 20 seconds has become difficult for most people to handle. The average person's concentration span is much shorter than it used to be. A lot of people regret this.

But this is how people are today. They don't read Dickens, with his six-line sentences. Harold Robbins, following Hemingway, got us accustomed to the six-word sentence. Here's a six-word sentence: This is how people are today. This is what we have to aim for.

It's not easy. Our education taught us to cope effortlessly with 40 word sentences. We lawyers tend to think in longer strands than most people. We use grammatical forms jurors don't often use themselves. We use subordinate clauses. We use parenthesis.

We have to learn *not* to use them. It takes practice. Focus on this. Start examining your own sentences. Count the words. Find out how many words your average sentence contains. If your personal word count is greater than 22 start working actively to cut it back.

We are aiming for a balance here. We don't want to sound stilted yet we want to make sure we are effortlessly understandable at all times. Let me give an illustration from an American setting. (America uses juries for just about anything you can think of, and opening a case in front of a civil jury is much more fun than appearing before judge alone. Quite apart from the pleasure the advocate can get out of it, the litigants seem to get a deeper sense of satisfaction out of a jury trial, and this is true even of the loser. Jury verdicts seem to put an end to disputes far more satisfyingly than decisions by judge alone.) Take an absolutely typical opening statement and see what the civil jury is so often subjected to.

'Ladies and gentlemen, I, as you know, represent the plaintiff in the case, Mrs Mary Snooks, the case arising out of a most unfortunate collision which occurred on Sunday, August the 9th, 1987, at the junction between Caminito del Playa and the Samantha Smith Boulevard in Santa Barbara between a light blue Cadillac 1980 Eldorado which was being driven by my client and a dark blue Toyota station wagon that was at the time being driven, with permission and consent, by the son of the defendant who was currently employed by him and was delivering some urgent printed material to a customer for his father.'

That is typical. And the lawyer has already lost his jury. They started to get anxious at about line four. The first thing they asked themselves was, 'Are we expected to *remember* all this?' The next question they asked themselves was, 'Are we expected to take this all in?'

As the lawyer went inexorably on they quietly began to panic. They realised it was quite beyond them to retain the detail, to follow the detail even – and they began to switch off. By the end of the sentence they were uncomfortable and out of their depth, and already they were subconsciously regarding the lawyer as someone who was making life difficult for them.

This clearly illustrates the need for the Keep It Simple Rule, but it also leads to the next obvious Golden Rule:

DETAIL IS DANGEROUS

It is one of the surest signs of the inept advocate that he loads down his factfinder with *far* too much detail. It's probably got something to do with the fact that when we learn to draft pleadings and indictments we are taught to include *all* necessary particulars. We are brainwashed into feeling guilty if we don't give sufficient detail: we are frightened of leaving out some essential element. We have also been trained to have an authority ready at our fingertips, a justification, to back up every utterance we make in court. Our trained professional instincts urge us to volunteer chapter and verse for just about everything.

Because this is the mould we are cast in, smothering the factfinder with too much detail is a very understandable impulse on the lawyer's part. But it's an impulse you must recognise and control, because *detail is dangerous to good advocacy.*

You see it again and again, and you see a glazed look come over the jury. If you overload them they won't *understand*, they won't *listen* and they will *resent you* bitterly.

How should that detail-festooned opening have been done? Something like this perhaps:

'Ladies and gentlemen, let me tell you what I expect the evidence to prove. This case is about a collision between two cars and what happened as a result. It was a summer's day a few years back. Mary Snooks, mother of two, was driving an old Cadillac. She knew the road well. As she came to a familiar crossing where *she* had the right of way, she saw a Toyota. This other car was approaching its stop line on Mary Snooks's left-hand side. But instead of stopping, instead of slowing down even, the Toyota came right out into the junction. And there was a collision. Bear with me a moment while I give you a few details about that collision and its results. Let me summarise for you, in as few words as possible, what you are likely to hear from the witnesses in this case. First, who was driving that other car?'

Right? Look carefully at what has been left out. See how much we were able to do without. There's no mention of the month when it happened. There's no mention of the day of the week or of the date. There's no mention of the names of the roads, the model of the Cadillac, the year it was built. These details *didn't matter. They just cluttered everything up.*

We haven't stripped out *all* the detail. We've left in enough for the jury to construct the clearest picture in their own mind, using their own imagination. And we've given them enough detail to imagine how *they* would have felt if they had been driving along that road.

But we have *eliminated everything we could do without*, everything that wasn't strictly necessary for our purpose. And what was that purpose? It was to tell them a story they would want to listen to and be interested in, while at the same time stating the facts in such a way as to start them feeling that our case was fair and reasonable and that the verdict we were suggesting was equally fair.

So when I offer you as a Golden Rule, *Avoid Detail*, you may feel the rule can be extended slightly:

WORK AT ELIMINATING EVERYTHING THAT CAN SAFELY BE ELIMINATED

Your case should be as lean as you can make it. It shouldn't carry an ounce of unnecessary weight.

Which brings us to a Golden Rule we have already met, when talking about the Dimension of Time, but a Rule we didn't actually put into words:

·   BE BRIEF!

Do not use up a minute more of your factfinder's time than is absolutely necessary. It works. It works incredibly well. You doubt this? I doubted it. We all doubted it. The Golden Rule *Be Brief!* sounds like an encouragement to chicken out, not to do your best for the client, not to do a thorough job. It's not true.

Being brief requires planning, real preparation, intensely concentrated thinking. Covering all the points you need to cover without a single wasted word, making the impact you need to make as economically as you possibly can, is anything but easy. Getting ready to do this successfully can be hard labour. But it works and I'll demonstrate to you why it works.

Imagine yourself sitting on a jury. The advocate stands up and does his opening. He tells you a story, a story that's easy to follow and that engages your interest. You can see very clearly why the case had to come to court. He's made you feel a wrong has been suffered that needs to be righted. But suddenly he's stopped. Just when you were comfortably settling in to the unexpectedly enjoyable business of listening to this interesting fellow – he's finished. *He has stopped before you've had enough.* He followed the rule of all good entertainment: *he left you wanting more.*

You are now in a state of looking forward to the next time that advocate gets to his feet. When he does he will have your total attention. But he does it again. Even before you settle in to really enjoying it, he's finished. And he does it again the time after that. He does it all the way through the trial. Then you come to his final speech and instead of being so brief, this time he gives you a little more. And even a little bit more is so gratifying.

By working the Brevity Rule in harness with the Tell Them a Story Rule in harness with the Avoid Detail Rule, this advocate has you sitting in rapt attention every time he opens his mouth. When you see it done properly it's a delight to behold, and the contrast with the ordinary, run-of-the-mill advocate is amazing.

There is one last rule I'd like to share with you under the general heading of Keeping Them Entertained. It's this:

PREPARE THEM FOR THE BORING BITS

There *are* trials without any boring bits but they are rare. Although you strive to keep your boring bits to a minimum you can rarely avoid them altogether. How do you hold the jury's attention during a barren patch, during an investigation of what are bound to be boring details? The lawcourt stops being good theatre at this point. Is there anything you can do about it?

It's surprisingly easy. All you have to do is warn them in advance and then, during the boring interlude, make the occasional reference to time. The factfinder doesn't expect a trial to be all plain sailing. Both judge and jury realise that work has to be done from time to time. As long as you make it clear that you *recognise* the barren patch and also make it clear that you are doing your best to get everybody through it as effortlessly as possible, you won't lose their attention and they won't hold it against you.

So tell them in advance:

'The time will come in this trial, ladies and gentlemen, when I'm going to have to ask you to give your keenest attention to some rather complicated figures. I'm sorry about this but it can't be avoided. I'll help you through them as best I can, and I can tell you now this shouldn't occupy more than a couple of hours of your time. But that's some way down the road yet, and I'll warn you when we get to it. Meanwhile . . .'

Preparing them for the boring bits is a specific application of a wider Golden Rule which says simply: *Prepare Them.* But can we come to that a little later? I'd like to finish with the theatre-courtroom comparison first. I want to deal for a moment or two with this thing called *Voice.*

This is something the actor studies carefully: we lawyers give it hardly any attention. We should. There are even members of the Bar out there whom juries have difficulty in hearing. Others have such heavy, booming voices that jurors cower before them. Both kinds are letting down the client. There are a few obvious Golden Rules relating to Voice. *First,*

KNOW YOUR AUDIBILITY

Be sure that you know how loudly you have to speak so as to be heard. Courts come in different shapes and sizes. Ceiling heights vary considerably. Some courts have sound-absorbing walls, some ring like the inside of a bell. If you haven't already done it, practise using your voice in as many different spaces as you can. Get your spouse or friend to tell you how easily you can be heard. Explore your range of loudness and softness. Very important is to discover how quietly you can talk while still being easy to hear. This is because the quieter and more conversational your tone in court the more effective you usually are.

The days of great oratory are over – at least for the time being. People respond more, these days, to the Peter Sissons kind of delivery – conversational, informative and fairly gentle – and knowing your own audibility at this end of your range is essential.

Next rule:

VARY YOUR PACE AND VARY YOUR TONE

If you don't you will sound boring, and if your voice sounds boring you undo most of the good you accomplished by putting all the other rules into operation. Listen to yourself on the tape recorder. If you can bear to, set up a video camera on yourself while in conversation with someone. Listen critically. Is your pace too fast? Even worse, is it too slow? What range of high and low do you cover? Is it nice to listen to? Is it comfortable? As I said very early on, we tend to be bashful about examining ourselves like this. Don't be. Other people are going to be examining you all the time in court. You don't want to be the last to know you have some irritating habit you could quite easily correct.

Next rule:

BE AWARE OF TIMING AND THE
POWER OF THE PAUSE

Ask theatre people what makes a great actor and most of them say, 'Timing'. Good advocates know how important it is. But the inexperienced are often so anxious to maintain continuity, to keep talking, to avoid silences, they overlook the question of timing altogether. Don't make this mistake. Don't ignore the dramatic impact that a pause can create. It's important to maintain your continuity but that doesn't mean you have to babble.

If you haven't much thought about this before, I'd suggest you look out for it in the better television presentations. The newscasters are usually good illustrations of the acceptable pace of delivery, and whatever you thought about him personally, Benny Hill was a master exponent of the power of the pause.

Before leaving the subject of Voice, let me pass on a hint:

BE TERRIBLY CAREFUL ABOUT RAISING
YOUR VOICE

For some reason I can't fully explain, when an advocate raises his voice in court people usually wonder, instinctively, what's gone wrong for him. It's probably to do with the fact that a raised voice usually signals anger or frustration. Whatever the reason, I've seen it again and again over the years. Raise your voice and they'll think something has gone wrong for you. So beware.

Dropping your voice, on the other hand, has exactly the opposite effect. As a means of emphasising something it works wonderfully. This is why it's so important to know the quiet end of your audibility levels.

Very well. That's all I want to say about the Golden Rules which arise out of the lawcourt as theatre. There are bound to be others. Try to formulate for yourself what they might be. What we come to now is the interesting stuff, the rules which emerge by examining *the psychology of advocacy*.

THE PSYCHOLOGY
OF ADVOCACY

The Psychology of Advocacy

Let's go right back for a moment to the first thing we talked about – the First Dimension of Advocacy. By the time we get to court we ought no longer to be digging for the truth: we are trying to get an *opinion* from our factfinder saying 'You win: the other side loses'. In civil claims we sometimes want another opinion as well. 'In our opinion your client ought to be compensated in the sum of such and such.' In criminal cases we want them to say 'In our opinion this case has or has not been proved beyond reasonable doubt'. In civil cases, 'It's our opinion that, on balance, this is the side that wins the contest'.

Of course there's a search for truth going on in a trial, but it's not the main objective. Watching and listening to the witnesses, the factfinder is bound to be on the lookout for the liar. But trials often end up – usually end up, indeed – without any liars being unmasked. What the factfinders normally have to do is decide which parts of the evidence they prefer. An advocate's job is to lead his or her factfinder to a *preference* and thus to an *opinion*.

It's obvious, isn't it, that preferences and opinions may be very firm and clearly held, or, on the other hand, not firm at all and anything but clear. We are not dealing with black-and-white, absolute things here. As long as we win their preference and their opinion we win the case. The point to be emphasised is that preferences and opinions are often fragile, delicate things.

Your factfinders may arrive at their preference and their opinion entirely as a result of *thinking*. But that's not very likely, is it? Even trained thinkers like us, in choosing between two conflicting witnesses, often ask ourselves what our gut reaction is. We think. Of course we think. But we also feel. The process of getting to a preference and an opinion involves both – thinking and feeling.

In a trial by judge alone you are before a trained thinker: here there may be more thinking than feeling involved in the search for preference and opinion. I say 'may be' because that isn't by any means certain. Judges are human too.

But with a jury, as with any kind of factfinder who doesn't have legal training – as, for example, the members of a court martial – you simply *must* work on the assumption that their feelings will be operating *at least* as much as their thinking while they work out their preferences and opinions.

If preferences and opinions can be fragile, delicate things, human feelings are undoubtedly the same. And these are the materials which we advocates have to work with.

THE MATERIALS OF ADVOCACY ARE FRAGILE

This isn't so much a Golden Rule as a fundamental truth that should be remembered at all times. Yet it's a truth that has never occurred to many advocates. You see lawyers behaving as if their factfinders had no feelings at all, whereas it is their feelings you should be reaching out to all the time.

Your job is to make them feel, as well as think, that they prefer your version. It is your task, in total honesty, to lead them to this. And if you take this as your starting-point all sorts of guidelines present themselves.

The first is surely obvious. You want to lead them: you want them to follow. Which will they follow more willingly, a person they like or a person they dislike?

So Psychological Golden Rule Number One:

BE LIKEABLE

At least be more likeable than your opponent. Leave the macho advocate where he belongs, on the television screen. The nice approach is infinitely more effective. When the nice advocate occasionally gets nasty – as very occasionally he may have to – the contrast is tremendous. If you are likeable, affable and kindly you will evoke all your factfinder's nicest feelings. They will want to believe you. Affability will carry you through all kinds of difficulty, and jurors have a disturbing tendency to find in favour of the lawyer they like. So work at it.

But be careful. Juries have an amazing nose for insincerity. If you just try to *act* nice they'll smell you out. The Golden Rule isn't 'Act likeable': it's '*Be likeable*'. If this involves rearranging bits of your personality, do it. If you need it, get help.

You see, the truth is that we all have a nicest side. It's that version of us our loved ones know, that version of us we share with people we really like. *This* is the version we ought to take to court. Instead, most lawyers put on a cloak of grim seriousness, solemnity, gravity, pomposity, and leave the real human being somewhere back at home. Coming across as utterly *real* and genuinely *nice* works wonders in court. Apart from anything else, it tends to be so different from the norm that the factfinder cannot help but notice and respond accordingly.

Now that's a simple rule. Let me give you a more subtle one. I think of it as the

SYMPATHY RULE

and since understanding and following this rule bring such guaranteed rewards I want to explain it carefully.

If you can convert a dozen unfamiliar people into a group who are sympathetic to you personally, you perform a wonderful service for your client. If they become sympathetic towards you a number of results will flow:

- They will listen willingly.
- They will put the kindest interpretation on what you say.
- They will feel reluctant to deny you what you ask.
- They will feel inclined to overlook your mistakes.

If you want the clearest example of what a sympathetic audience can be like, think back to an infants' school play. There sits the audience of parents, hardly breathing, as their darling children appear on stage. Every mistake is forgiven, the tiny little voices break an otherwise perfect silence in which you could hear a pin drop, and the energy willing them to succeed is so real you could almost photograph it.

It's an extreme example but compare it with, say, a meeting of angry shareholders determined to have the chairman and managing director off the board and preferably out of the country. When I talk about sympathy, this is the kind of thing I'm referring to. The infants' school play and the shareholders' meeting are opposite ends of the scale.

As an advocate, which end would you prefer to be nearer? The forgiving, giving end, or the truculent, hostile end? It's amazing how many lawyers choose the rough end – as a result of their ignorance and sheer insensitivity. They've never paused to think about *sympathy* between advocate and factfinder. It's never occurred to them. As a result their clients suffer.

It's obvious that a sympathetic judge and jury are better for your case than the other kind, so is it just a question of luck or can you do something about this? Strange to say, you actually can get a flow of sympathy going between you and your factfinder and the technique for doing it is surprisingly easy.

Take a little time to play a mental game with yourself. Try to imagine what it must be liké to be sitting where your judge is sitting, seeing what she's seeing, hearing what she's hearing. Try to put yourself as completely as you can in her position. Do exactly the same with your jurors – every one of them. Do it as they come into court at the outset and do it now and again right through the trial. Imagine yourself into the individual's skin: get behind his or her eyes. It takes virtually no effort, yet it undoubtedly accomplishes something. This simple exercise puts you in far greater sympathy with them and, somehow or other, they are subconsciously aware of it. The result is they give sympathy back to you.

I make no claim to understanding how this exchange of energy takes place. All I can tell you is that the technique works. Try it for yourself. You'll soon find it prevents you from making all sorts of mistakes. You won't say or do things that get their backs up. You won't, as so many lawyers do, get into a confrontation with your factfinder. You'll have a much smoother ride with them.

And you'll be less in need of the next and vitally important *Golden Rule.* I think of it as

NEWTON'S RULE

but it can equally well be thought of as

THE RULE OF EQUALS AND OPPOSITES

Let's return for a moment to what I just said. If you pay attention to the Sympathy Rule you won't get into a *confrontation* with your factfinder. Most advocates go barging into confrontations with the factfinder as a matter of course. They create them all the time:

'You can't convict my client, ladies and gentlemen!'
('Can't we now?' think the jury.)

'You couldn't possibly . . .', says the lawyer.
('Oh no?' say their faces.)

'You will have to . . ..'
('Will we, now?')

The rule is simple. You push and they'll push back. You pull and they'll resist. You demand and they'll refuse you. You insist and they'll turn you down. Newton's law of motion isn't just a scientific law: it's an accurate description of human response as well. An action almost invariably produces its equal and opposite reaction, and it's one of the most important Golden Rules of Advocacy.

If you think intently about this you will see how to avoid trouble. Instead of demanding you *invite*. Instead of telling, you *suggest*. You don't *insist* they look at something: you *suggest* they might find it helpful if they did. You don't pull, you lead, and you lead gently. Stick and carrot have no place in advocacy: it's exclusively carrot.

The more you think about Newton's Rule the better advocate you become. It is the most important rule of all when it comes to the question of *persuasion*. Not only does it keep you out of trouble: it can be used to tremendous advantage.

'You probably won't feel that this is terribly important, ladies and gentlemen' will focus their attention remarkably. If you say something like, 'I'm sorry, I'm not putting this at all clearly', you'll almost certainly get their unspoken response: 'No. Go on. We're understanding you perfectly.'

This isn't a subtle advocate's trick. It is a rule of human behaviour. If you know it and think about it you'll relate to your factfinder far better, you won't offend them and they'll listen far more willingly.

This is such an important rule that I feel it's worth giving you a slightly fuller illustration. Let's take a common situation that arises, again, in a criminal case – they often furnish the best illustrations. The line the defence are taking is that the police are telling a pack of lies and that all of their testimony is a fabrication. Macho advocates normally slam into the jury in their final speeches, telling them that the police are lying, that the whole thing is a travesty, that they *can't* convict etc., etc.

Do you know what the average juror feels when she hears that? The average juror has never had a brush with the law. The only time she had a real encounter with a police officer was when she got her name taken for a traffic offence she *had* committed, and although he stopped her the officer was polite and even a bit regretful. To the average juror the police are the saviours, the people who protect. Even today, after all the shame that has fallen upon our system of criminal justice, this is still, generally speaking, the public attitude.

If you insist to your average jury that the police are the villains, you go against their belief system. It disturbs them: they don't want to

think that. If you ignore Newton's Rule at this point you are likely
to create a confrontation. But if you do think about Newton's Rule,
you almost certainly avoid the danger. How about this as an
illustration?

'Ladies and gentlemen, one unhappy thing about this case is that
I've had to suggest the police have been deceiving us. Not a pretty
idea, is it? Not something any of us want to admit, the thought that
the police who look after this community of ours, who make it safe
for us to sleep at night, might have among them officers who are
willing to lie to judge and jury so as to get someone convicted,
officers who are prepared to stretch and bend the law. We'd rather
not think about it. Far easier to turn our backs on the possibility
as we turn away from other unpleasant thoughts. Shall we do that?
Shall we say "He's a police officer: he couldn't possibly have been
lying!"? Or shall we look together, carefully, to see whether
someone's been trying to pull the wool over your eyes?'

There's no risk of confrontation there. We haven't pushed once, we
haven't pulled, and we haven't trampled on their natural prejudices.
Far from it. *We've adopted their prejudices as our own.* We've been
talking their language and they know it. We avoided all equal and
opposite reactions until the end, and then we used them in our favour.
'Shall we turn our backs on this possibility?' we asked. What can the
jury silently reply to that except, 'Of course not'. 'Shall we assume
. . .?' brings an almost automatic equal and opposite: 'No'.

And we also suggested that someone may have been trying to pull the
wool over their eyes. What is their reaction bound to be – 'Well,
they're not going to succeed!'

Think Newton. Let Newton become part of you. He'll keep you out
of all kinds of trouble and make a real advocate out of you.

Did you notice another thing we were doing in that little illustration?
We were placing ourself firmly on the same side as the jury. It wasn't
a case of advocate here and jury over there. It was a case of *we*, not
you. Shall *we* assume? Shall *we* turn our backs on it? Were lies being
told to *us*? It's an example of the next Golden Rule in operation:

INCLUDE THE FACTFINDER

or

THE RULE OF THE FIRST PERSON PLURAL

Think *we*, never *they*. The witnesses tell *us* not *you*. 'And what were we told by Mr Snooks? You remember what he said don't you?' Get this idea firmly established in your mind, and you'll begin running in harness with your jurors and probably with your judge as well. When you are questioning a witness you'll remember for whose benefit your questions are being asked – your factinder's. Instead of bald questions you find you are extending invitations. 'Would you tell these ladies and gentlemen what happened then?' 'Tell his honour and the jury where you were when this happened'.

You mustn't overdo it. It's like any ingredient that makes things tastier: it has to be used in the right quantities. But it should always be there. The factfinders must always feel included rather than dispassionate umpires sitting on the sidelines.

The next rule was fleetingly mentioned some time ago but let's examine it now. It's the Golden Rule which says, quite simply:

PREPARE THEM

We don't need to spend much time on this because once stated it's obvious. If you have weaknesses in your case – and *all* cases have weaknesses – then make sure you are the first to mention them. Get to your difficulties before anyone else does. You will handle them so much more sympathetically than your opponent. If you have an unattractive client or unattractive witnesses don't let the jury discover this for themselves. Tell them in advance and as carefully as you can. Use a little Newton if possible. If you have witnesses with really weak points in their testimony, make certain that you get to those weaknesses in direct examination. Do not leave them there for your opponent to make hay with. He'll try to do that anyway but spoil it for him in advance. Take away the element of surprise. Aim to make the jury feel, when he gets there, 'Oh, that. Yes, we were told about that.'

You can say virtually anything in a court of law provided you lay the right kind of foundation for it. Prepare your way properly and you can exclaim obscenities! No one will bat an eyelid.

Let me move quickly on to a rule which summarises a lot of what we've already been discussing. It's the Golden Rule which tells you:

ALWAYS AIM TO BE THE HONEST GUIDE

Early on, when I was talking about the Third Dimension of Advocacy – people don't like lawyers – I recommended that you find a totally honest, totally sincere way of presenting your case. You are not a hired gun, prepared to do anything for the right price. You are a professional with professional responsibilities and professional pride. By the time the factfinder has spent 20 minutes in your company they should be beginning to feel, not only that you are honest, but that they can trust you. More than that, they should already have started to get the feeling that they can trust you completely, that you are not going to dupe them in any way. By the end of the first day these people, who were strangers in the morning, must go away knowing that there was at least one person in that courtroom that they'd feel safe buying a second-hand car from.

I can't give you a technique for accomplishing this. There's no substitute for real sincerity and real honesty and real niceness. If you hold on to the Golen Rules we've been discussing and are sincere and honest you'll establish yourself as an Honest Guide. What I *can* do is point out three danger areas, then give you three positive hints. First the dont's.

One: DON'T ASK THEM TO BELIEVE
                     THE UNBELIEVABLE

If you press them to accept something that is beyond them, your credibility will vanish in a puff of smoke. Any good you may have accomplished so far will be undone. You will have become a tredecator – a clock that strikes 13.

Two: WHEN THERE IS A WEAK POINT
                     IN YOUR CASE DON'T PRETEND

THAT IT ISN'T A WEAK POINT.
ADMIT IT AND SHOW THEM HOW
YOU STILL OUGHT TO SUCCEED
DESPITE THAT WEAKNESS

Three: DON'T MISQUOTE THE EVIDENCE
IN ANY WAY AT ALL AND DON'T
PUT A SLICK INTERPRETATION
ON ANY PART OF IT

Now three positive hints:

One: MAKE SURE THAT YOU ALWAYS
COME ACROSS AS BEING
ABSOLUTELY FAIR

Two: KEEP YOUR OBJECTIONS
TO A MINIMUM

Let's think about this for a moment. Every time a lawyer objects to something she risks making the jury wonder what she is trying to conceal from them. 'What are they keeping from us? Why?' Of course there are times when you have to object – either to the evidence that is being called for, or to the form of the question, or to something your opponent may be saying or doing.

So you have to make a rapid judgment. You have to ask yourself 'How important is this? Must I really object? Is it worth the risk that the jury will wonder what I'm keeping from them?' Sometimes you have to think very fast: it's not always an easy balancing process. But if you work to the principle 'Don't unless you have to' and keep in mind the dangers of objections, you won't go flinging them around for the fun of it.

And just on further comment on objections. It's usually a good idea to

SEEM RELUCTANT WHEN YOU MAKE THEM

The Rambo-type objector is great on television.

My final hint for preserving your Honest Guide status is this:

Three: TAKE GREAT CARE
GETTING YOUR JURY OUT OF COURT

There are times in every trial when things have to be discussed in their absence. Anything that involves admissibility is dealt with in open court but with the jury outside.

Being given a break in the corridor, where they can stretch their legs or perhaps have a quick cigarette is something no jury objects to – provided they don't feel something is being kept from them or that they are being excluded from something interesting.

The inexperienced advocate often does himself harm at this point. He stands up and asks for the jury to be sent out of court in such a way that they can't help wondering what they'll be missing. The Honest Guide, on the other hand, says something like this:

'My Lord, there's a question of law I need your ruling on at this point. You may think the jury could stretch their legs while we deal with it?'

Don't you feel that invites their gratitude rather than their curiosity? If the judge is bluntly insensitive and says 'You want the jury out of court, Mr Snooks?', you reply:

'There's no need for them to sit through a technical legal discussion, my Lord. I think it's right they should be excused at this point.'

Any form of words will do, as long as you are aware of the need to take care.

That's all I want to say about the Honest Guide. Just remember that if you really want to be an advocate, you have no choice but to become, and remain, an Honest Guide.

There is only one other Golden Rule I want to discuss under the Psychology of Advocacy heading, but before I do let me give you half a dozen short hints – tips that ought to make life easier for you.

DEMONSTRATE YOUR COMPETENCE
TO YOUR JUDGE AS EARLY AS POSSIBLE

Quote a section of some statute or a scrap of case law. Any little thing like this will do and it sends a signal. Judges are so burdened by lawyers who really don't know their job. A sign from you that you probably aren't one of them gets the right energy going.

PRACTISE LISTENING INTENTLY

In court we are so concerned with what we are saying and how we are saying it, we often forget to listen as carefully as we should. It sounds silly, I know, but it really is a danger, espcially during our first few trials. We are so wrapped up in the difficulties of getting out our questions and feel such a sense of relief when we actually launch one, we often don't pay full attention to the answer. Intent listening isn't easy. It has to be practised. Practise it.

Next, a hint to get you out of trouble. Although you'll be doing your best to keep it simple and use short sentences, from time to time you are going to get lost. Your sentence is going to get longer and longer until you lose your way. Most inexperienced advocates get flustered at this point because they don't know what to do. So it gets worse. The secret is to

STOP DEAD IN YOUR TRACKS

As soon as you realise your sentence is a failure, stop. Say something like: 'I'm not putting this clearly. Let me start again.' Nobody minds. If *you've* got lost you can be sure *they* have, and they'll be grateful to you for taking the load off them as well as off yourself. You can start again without any sense of failure. We all get lost from time to time.

Next: remember the rule about not repeating yourself. It's important. If you repeat yourself and they got the point first time, they'll feel you are insulting their intelligence. But how about those occasions when you feel you really must say it again?

Tell them you are going to do it. Let *them* know that *you* know you are doing it. 'Forgive me for repeating myself, ladies and gentlemen, but it's such an important point . . . .' If you give advance warning you won't cause offence. Nevertheless, remember the rule and:

USE REPETITION VERY SPARINGLY

There are, however, two important exceptions to the *Don't Repeat Yourself* rule. One can be thought of as:

THE COFFIN NAIL EXCEPTION

If, in cross-examination, you are lucky enough to get a witness on the run and you have a list of things which you know he is going to have to admit, then you can use one, repeating, form of question over and over again, driving the nails into the lid of the coffin.

> 'You knew that so and so, didn't you Mr Witness?'
> 'Yes.'
> 'Very well. Knowing what you did, did you this?'
> 'No.'
> 'Knowing what you did, did you that?'
> 'No.'
> 'Knowing what you did, did you the other?'
> 'No.'

You can get a slow drum-beat going if you do it right, and juries love it, their heads turning from you to the witness and back again like the crowd at Wimbledon.

You can think of the other time to repeat yourself as:

THE MARK ANTONY EXCEPTION

In your final speech (and in the rarest of cases in your opening) you might be able to find a short form of words that you can repeat like a theme. 'For Brutus is an honourable man, so are they all, all honourable men.' Antony repeated that five times before Brutus got up and left.

If you can find such a theme, use it. But make sure it's worth hearing again and again. Don't try it out on your factfinder without having tried it out first on your spouse and/or friends and, preferably, on a teenager or two. When it works it works wonderfully.

We just encountered the word 'theme' – a kind of tune that can be played repeatedly in your final speech. 'Theme' also has another meaning, for the American lawyer anyway, and I'd like to deal with this briefly if only to point the contrast between here and there.

Remember that in the United States most civil cases are tried with a jury. It's a right guaranteed by the constitution: 20 dollars or more in dispute, and either side can demand one. When jurors are called into the box, counsel on both sides are allowed to ask them questions before deciding whether to exercise the right of challenge. This questioning of jurors – *voir dire* – doesn't usually take more than half a day, but during that time you've talked to all your jurors and you have discovered quite a lot about them. They have become *people*, individuals, with their own lives, their own careers and their own fund of knowledge and awareness. They are by this time very different from the total strangers you start out with in an English jury-box.

When you open your case to these people, you try to explain what it's about as succinctly as you can. You aim to give it to them in a nutshell, encapsulating your case in one short, easy-to-remember sentence.

'This is a case of a cynical corporation putting profit ahead of public safety.'

'This is a story of an electricity generating company being so inefficient, uncaring and unaware that they committed environmental barbarity over hundreds of square miles of your county.'

'This plaintiff is trying it on, exaggerating the results of her accident and gambling that your natural sympathies will prevent you from seeing through to the truth.'

You couldn't do this in front of an English judge. You couldn't open with a ringing declaration of what your case is really about. He'd wonder what had hit him. In English civil trials there is very rarely a jury to address. The judge will have read the pleadings and the correspondence, and will be expecting you to call your first witness.

Yet having an American-style theme to your case, even if you have to dilute the way you use it, has distinct advantages. If you have taken the trouble to define your theme, it will focus your presentation wonderfully, quite apart from sharpening your own awareness of the case. Even though you can't use 'theme of the case' as an American lawyer would, it's useful to have a theme and to know exactly what it is. Let me steal a short section from a presentation by Brian Monaghan, one of California's most successful plaintiff's attorneys:

> Keeping in mind that every piece of evidence in the trial should relate to the whole, it is absolutely vital to develop a theme which encapsulates the theory of the case to which all evidence should relate. Some examples: *Sanchez* v *Bay General Hospital* (1981) 116 Cal App 3d 776, a hospital negligence case in which the plaintiff's deceased mother received relatively routine cervical neurosurgery and was released from the recovery room to the post-surgery floor in stable condition but then was allowed to deteriorate to the point where she experienced brain death through aspiration of her own vomit. She remained in a vegetative state for several months and eventually expired when a tracheotomy tube was allowed to wear through bone, muscle and tissue into the innominate artery because it was unattended. In that case the theme was 'They ignored her to death – *twice*'.
>
> In *Bigboy* v *County of San Diego* (1984) 154 Cal App 3d 397, a case involving a dangerous condition of a public road, the passenger in the right front seat of the car was ejected when it lost control on a dangerous unsigned rural road. The theme in that case was, 'Dana will be a paraplegic for the next 45 years because the county *wouldn't spend 200 bucks* to correct a condition that they knew was one of the most dangerous in San Diego'. While this theme is longer than I would prefer, it focuses first on the strongest parts of the case – the permanency of injuries and the minimal costs of correcting the problem.
>
> In a case involving a real estate purchase-leaseback-and-sale scam, the theme was, 'Mr R—— was a foreclosure savior who himself became a millionaire in two short years'.

Next: how should you plan the strategy of your case? How can you know what witnesses to call? How can you keep track of everything?

How can you anticipate the difficulties you are likely to meet. Here is the original Golden Rule of Planning and it solves all those problems. As soon as you have an approximate idea of what a new case is about:

SIT DOWN AND WRITE YOUR FINAL SPEECH

Yes, your final speech. Sit down and write what you would have to say so as to be confident of winning the verdict. Don't worry at this stage if bits of it are fiction. Just from what you know of the case, write out your ideal final speech.

Then read it. See how well the available evidence supports it. At once you will see the gaps, the missing bits. Trying to close those gaps is the preparation of your case. When you think you are getting close, perform another exercise:

SIT DOWN AND WRITE YOUR *OPPONENT'S* FINAL SPEECH

This will concentrate your focus still more sharply on what you still need to do by way of preparation and on the weak points you will have to reach and deal with before anyone else does.

When all this preparation has been done, sit down and

PERFECT *YOUR* FINAL SPEECH

This is the blueprint of your trial. It becomes a record of your progress through the case, a shopping list of all you have to do, a foolproof checklist. The evidence you need and the way you need to present it stares straight at you from this final plan. It's a great method and I commend it to you.

So what is this last Golden Rule before we turn to the examination of witnesses? It is the rule which tells you all the way through trial, but particularly in your final argument, to

SHOW THEM THE WAY HOME

I had an attorney telephone me some time ago. He had been to one of my seminars and he'd been musing over the rules. 'You know,' he said, 'this is *the* Golden Rule. It subsumes all the others. As long as you remember to be likeable, *Show them the Way Home* contains everything else. It's the supreme rule of advocacy.

I don't know if he's right. I don't know if you can say that about any one Golden Rule. I do agree there are half a dozen standing out from all the rest – Entertain Them, Tell them a Story, the Sympathy Rule, the Honest Guide, Prepare Them, Newton's Rule – but can you pick just one and say it is more important than the others? I don't know. These fundamental rules are like the major branches of an oak tree. And I told him this. 'Ah,' he said, 'but *Show them the Way Home* is the trunk of the tree itself!'

And in that sense, he was right. It *is* like the trunk of the tree out of which everything else ought to grow. Let me try to explain it.

Show them the Way Home. What do we mean by 'Home'? It's the verdict we are asking for, the goal we are aiming at, the objective, the only reason we are in court. Everything we have done has been done for this. It's all been done in order to get that verdict. That's 'Home'.

Show them the 'Way'. What do we mean by 'the Way'? This is the heart of it.

Your factfinder, whether judge or jury, arbitrator or referee, usually starts out as a complete stranger to your case. They come like travellers in a new land. Somewhere in this country is the city you want to take them to, the city called *Verdict*. You know their journey to that city could be a difficult one. If this weren't so you wouldn't be in court. And you have an opponent who wants to take them somewhere else altogether. Both of you are there, as the travellers arrive like tourists wondering what lies ahead of them, and from the outset you are like two tour-operators in competition for those tourists.

The brilliant advocate grabs them all, there and then. He paints them a picture of an easy, enjoyable journey, through interesting countryside, over smooth, paved roads. He sells them his city as a place where they'll feel content to be, a place worth having arrived at, a place where they'll be so welcome, a place where they'll be more than just tourists, a place where they'll experience a new and exciting sensation: the pleasure of bringing *right* where before there was *wrong*.

And off they all go, with the other tour-guide chasing along behind, desperately trying to catch up and never even coming close.

Unofficial statistics, so I am told, show that a jury often decides on its verdict, after it's heard the *opening*! The mind-set they get into at that point stays with them all the way through. Unless there is a catastrophe in the evidence they never swerve. They choose the guided tour they prefer and stick with it. It happens. I've seen it done and I've done it myself. I've had it done to me.

'The Way' to that city has to be attractive and as smooth and easy as you can possibly make it. There are bound to be obstacles and difficulties and *it is your job to know in advance what they are and where they are*. Before ever the travellers arrive you must have planned their journey so as to take them around the obstacles and so as to minimise the difficulties. Your tour must be designed to drive them through countryside that will engage their interest and attention. The places where you give them a rest-break should be thought about with care, the route should be chosen so that a gentle stretch leads to a dramatic vista where they can ooh and ah before coming to another easy-going stage in the journey.

You can see what that attorney meant when he said that *Show them the Way Home* subsumes other Golden Rules. *Entertain Them* is in there. The *Honest Guide* and *Be Likeable* are obviously there as well. So is *Preparation*. Once you see what *Show them the Way Home* is all about, it's obvious that it runs all the way through your advocacy.

But let's be specific. We can see the way it applies generally. Let's have a couple of examples of the rule in action.

Focus on two words: *easy* and *difficult*.

For the average human being, taking decisions is difficult, far more difficult than the average advocate realises. If you have any aspirations at all to being a lawyer you are, by nature, more decisive than the average citizen. Most people prefer to have their decisions taken for them. If they are put on the rack of not knowing what to do for the best they often get agitated and distressed.

Your job is to remove their difficulties. Your task is to leave them with a decison they don't really have to take at all – because it takes itself. You should be aiming to make it a foregone conclusion by the time they go off to deliberate their verdict. If you are doing it right you should be striving, from first to last, to *make it easy for them*.

It seems, doesn't it, as if I'm stating the obvious? Of course we should be striving to make it *easy* for·our factfinder to come down on our side. But, again, it seems as if most advocates have never so much as thought about this. I once watched a member of the Bar make sure his client went to prison. It was at the sentencing stage of the case. His client had pleaded guilty at the outset but all other defendants had made a fight of it and been acquitted by the jury. Because the judge had seen the real villains go free, he clearly felt sorry for the only fellow who had admitted his guilt. The only difficulties in 'the Way' to a very light and lenient sentence were, first, it was quite a serious offence, and second, the man had two previous convictions from several years before.

Defence counsel could have said something like this:

'Serious offence, my Lord, *and* it comes on top of two convictions some time back. These matters may make it difficult for your Lordship to pass a moderate sentence. But I'm in your Lordship's hands. I wasn't here throughout the trial and your Lordship knows far better than I can what justice requires in this case.'

That would have accomplished a number of things:

● It would have been a public acknowledgement, made on behalf of the defendant and in his presence, that his offence was a serious one.
● It would have been an acknowledgement of the fact that the defendant had a criminal record and that this wasn't something that could be just brushed aside.

- These acknowledgements would have removed a difficulty all judges face when wanting to be lenient – the risk that a light sentence will make it look as if the court didn't regard the offence as a serious one.
- They would have removed another difficulty. The court cannot ignore a defendant's criminal record. If a judge passes a light sentence it can seem as if that record got overlooked. Either way the public might be disturbed.

But with the kind of words used in our hypothetical we are placing ourselves firmly on the same side as the judge. By acknowledging the problems standing in the way of a lenient sentence, by voicing them in public, we remove the fear that anyone will think the offence wasn't serious. We remove the fear that anyone will think the criminal record got overlooked. Simply by telling the judge we know about his difficulties we diminish those difficulties.

And did you notice the use of *Newton's Rule*? 'These matters may make it difficult for your Lordship to pass a moderate sentence'. What is the equal and opposite reaction to that? If he's inclined to be lenient – as this judge was – his reaction could well be 'Try me!' or, 'Yes indeed, but you watch how I handle it!'

But what did defence counsel representing this defendant actually do? He made the judge's difficulties worse. He stood up in public and airily told the court this wasn't a serious offence at all. It was really terribly unimportant. Then he told us that the defendant's previous criminal record should be completely ignored because it had all happened years ago. Then he said it all over again.

I remember watching the judge's face. At first he looked bewildered, then angry, then hardly able to control himself. He was one of the nicer judges and he clearly wanted to pass a lenient sentence. But if he had been lenient after this fellow's presentation it would have looked as if he was agreeing with the nonsense that had been said to him. He passed a sentence of two years imprisonment. Had it not been for the lawyer, the defendant would have been let off on probation.

Not knowing *Show them the Way Home* can lose cases which might otherwise have been won. I got the verdict in a civil trial once, not because I had a stronger case but because my opponent broke the rule horribly. All the evidence was in and it was finely balanced. There had been six or seven witnesses on either side, and there wasn't much to choose between them. Since I was for the plaintiff I was afraid I hadn't satisfied my burden of proof and I was getting ready for the verdict to go against me.

Then came a gift from the Gods. My opponent in his closing argument told the judge – we had no jury – that all my witnesses had been lying. They had been trying to deceive the court. They were all dishonest.

Just think about the difficulties that placed in the way of the judge. If he gave the verdict to my opponent it would appear he was agreeing with him. He took the view, as I did, that all the witnesses had been doing their best and there was no intentional misleading. Now he was being asked to brand these people as liars. In rushed *Newton* and the judge reacted accordingly. What had been a finely balanced case now tipped in my favour. In his judgment his Lordship specifically found that the plaintiff's witnesses had not been lying and that, indeed, he preferred their testimony to that of the other side. Case over.

These are two fairly blatant examples, I agree. *Show them the Way Home* is usually a subtler thing altogether. And techniques as such aren't needed to put this Golden Rule into operation. If you focus on the necessity for doing everything you can to remove their difficulties you'll almost certainly do it right. Take time to think about your factfinder's difficulties. Only then can you try to do something about them.

There, anyway, is the last of the Golden Rules I offer you – Golden Rules which apply to *all* advocacy. If you think about them, merely bear them in mind, your advocacy will almost inevitably be of a superior quality. And when it comes to the question of examining witnesses you'll find you already know a great many do's and don'ts.

So let's turn to that now, the examination of witnesses.

THE EXAMINATION
OF WITNESSES

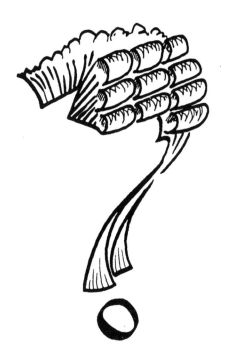

The Examination of Witnesses

Some years ago, during an air journey, I came across a short story in a magazine. I tore out a page and later got a fragment of it typed out:

Suddenly there was tension in the air. He didn't understand it. She stood across the room from him, her eyes blazing.

'Oh you!' she said, 'Your trouble is you're a lawyer! You always say things in such a way that the way is more important than what you are saying.'

'What have I said, for God's sake?' he pleaded.

'That's the whole point!' she flashed. 'It's not what you say, it's the way you say it. You say things and ask things as if you've thought out in advance the answer you want to hear, and your question always leads to you getting that answer.' She was talking fast and hotly now. 'Sometimes I don't know if you mean what you say or if you are just pulling strings to make me say something.'

'Give me an example,' he said, abashed.

'There you go again,' she retorted. And she swung around and vanished through the door, slamming it behind her.

Whoever the lady was in the story, she clearly knew one of the disadvantages of living with an advocate, and she put her finger right on the first and most important Golden Rule of Examining Witnesses. Let me repeat her words:

You've thought out in advance the answer you want to hear, and your question always leads to you getting that answer.

It must be hard, living with a competent advocate, because she has described exactly what we do. It's what we have to do – think out in advance the answer we want, then frame our questions so as to get that answer and only that answer.

Remember yet again our First Dimension. By the time we are in trial we are no longer on a search for the truth, but an opinion in our favour. The rules of evidence set strict limits on what the witnesses may say and what they may be asked. And yet, it is on what the witnesses do say that the case will be decided.

Your success or failure depends on *what* they say and *how* they say it. Focus intently on that. It's such a simple truth it tends to be overlooked.

It is the advocate's job to *control* what they say and how they say it. The lawyer who can't control these two variables is as dangerous as a driver who can't control his car, a pilot who can't control his aircraft, a dentist who can't control his drill. It is you who are in control and nobody else.

The First Golden Rule of Examining Witnesses is:

THINK CONTROL

The woman in the story was absolutely right:

KNOW WHAT YOU WANT THEM TO SAY
THEN MAKE THEM SAY IT

This is the secret of all successful examination of witnesses. This is your fundamental objective. Let this truth flow into you, sink into you and become part of you. This is the secret of how to exercise the *control* you must exercise.

It will almost certainly affect your private life – as it affected the life of the lawyer in the story. Once you get into the habit of knowing what you want to hear then getting the other person to say it, you'll find the habit almost impossible to break. When wives or husbands complain, 'Why can't you stop talking like a lawyer?', they don't actually mean that. What they really mean is, 'Why can't you stop *thinking* like a lawyer?' It's difficult. As you grow in skill as an examiner of witnesses you run the risk of becoming a lousy conversationalist. If you aren't careful you'll find yourself pulling people's strings and making them say what you want them to say in everyday life as well as in court. Beware of this. It can ruin relationships.

For we all have strings. We are all puppets in the hands of the right questioner. Even we, with all our education, can be led by the right series of questions. Those of you who find time to watch television may have seen a comedy series called 'Yes Minister'. I want to quote a snatch from this. A senior mandarin is explaining to a junior mandarin how to get any result you want from a public opinion survey. They are talking about reintroducing national service:

'Now Bernard, a nice young lady comes up to you with a clipboard. Obviously you want to create a good impression. You don't want to look like a fool, do you?'
'No.'
'So she starts asking you some questions. Are you worried about the number of young people without jobs?'
'Yes.'
'Are you worried about the rise in crime among teenagers?'
'Yes.'
'Do you think there's a lack of discipline in our comprehensive schools?'
'Yes.'
'Do you think young people welcome some authority and leadership in their lives?'
'Yes.'
'Do you think they respond to a challenge?'
'Yes.'
'Would you be in favour of reintroducing national service?'
'Uh – Well, I suppose I might be.'
'Yes or no?'
'Yes.'

'Of *course* you would Bernard. After all you've already told me you can hardly say no to that. . . . . Alternatively the young lady can get the opposite result.'
'How?'
'Mr Wooley, are you worried about the danger of war?'
'Yes.'
'Do you think there's a danger in giving young people guns and teaching them how to kill?'
'Yes.'
'Do you think it's wrong to force people to take up arms against their will?'
'Yes.'
'Would you oppose the reintroduction of national service?'
'Yes!!'
'There you are, you see, Bernard. You are the perfect balanced sample!'

Notice the following:

● The questioner knows exactly what she wants the witness to say.
● She arrives there by a *series* of questions.
● Each question in that series is almost guaranteed to get the individual answer she wants.

This is how any examination should be built. It doesn't matter if it's an examination of your own witness or a cross-examination.

EVERY EXAMINATION SHOULD CONSIST OF A SERIES OF OBJECTIVES

Aim to get the witness to agree to A, B and C and then, *as a consequence*, D. You must know in advance exactly what A, B, C and D are. You must know exactly what you want the witness to say – or to agree with.

Think of it, if you like, as a goods train – a series of wagons. Each one is an objective. Each one is a series of questions leading to the *answer you want*. Think out in advance the answer you want to hear and make your questions lead to you getting that answer. When you get it, move on to the next wagon.

Decide in advance with every individual witness what your overall objective is. If it's your own witness your objective is probably to draw out the story of what happened. If it's your own expert your objective is to bring out his opinion and his reasons for it. If it's an adverse witness you'll have other overall objectives which we'll come to shortly. But know exactly what they are.

Knowing this, you can then break it down into your goods train of individual objectives and work at them one by one, wagon by wagon.

Deal with them all – each individual objective as well as your overall objective – by thinking, 'If this, then that. If such and such, then so and so.' Design your questions so as to bring out this, this and this, then invite the witness to tell you or agree with what must follow as a result. And what follows as a result is the very form of words you want to hear.

If you go about your examination like this – with every wagon containing the answer you wanted together with the reasons why you got that answer – you will accomplish something very special: to your factfinder your advocacy will seem *irresistible*. Why? Because your factfinder will have followed you every step of the way. And if you can be irresistible you are likely to win their opinion.

If you do it this way – knowing your overall and individual objectives, working on each wagon in turn, and demonstrating as you go along *why* you are getting the answers you are getting – then, surprisingly enough, you shouldn't find it difficult examining witnesses. The reason why lawyers are afraid of the task, and why so many of them are so bad at it, is that they don't know what they are doing and they've never been given a blueprint to work to. Analysed out like this, it's a careful, step-by-step operation that no one need be afraid of.

But it needs an awful lot of preparation. It needs intensive thinking about. Planning a good examination can take a lot of time. Realise this and allow for it in your timetable if you possibly can. Don't feel inadequate if it doesn't come together quickly. Devising your series of questions which guarantee the answers you want is as important as anything in the case. It doesn't require vast skill or any kind of genius but it does require careful thought and sometimes a lot of it.

When you are dealing with the examination of your own client you have an obvious advantage. You can prepare her and together you can rehearse the whole thing. The rules permit it and, if you stick to total honesty in everything you do there is absolutely no objection, moral or otherwise, to having a word-perfect presentation ready for court.

When it comes to cross-examination, such rehearsing is impossible. But exactly the same Golden Rules apply. Know what you want the witness to say and get her to say it. Know your objectives and plan your series of questions with precision. This way you never lose control. But we'll come to cross-examination. What other Golden Rules are there, relating to the examination of witnesses generally?

The first thing to say is that we have already met most of the Rules for the Examination of Witnesses:

BE BRIEF

ENTERTAIN THEM

TELL THEM A STORY

UTMOST SINCERITY

DON'T SOUND LIKE A LAWYER

BEWARE OF REPEATING YOURSELF

DON'T PUT WORDS INTO THE MOUTH
OF YOUR OWN WITNESS

EYE CONTACT

GIVE THEM SOMETHING TO LOOK AT

BE LIKEABLE

THINK WE NOT THEY

GET TO YOUR WEAK POINTS
BEFORE YOUR OPPONENT

AVOID DETAIL

KEEP IT SIMPLE

THINK BEGINNING, MIDDLE AND END

LISTEN INTENTLY – PARTICULARLY TO
THE ANSWERS TO YOUR OWN QUESTIONS

VARY YOUR PACE AND VARY YOUR TONE

REMEMBER THE SYMPATHY RULE

ALWAYS APPEAR TO BE ABSOLUTELY FAIR

NEVER FORGET TO SHOW THEM THE WAY HOME

All these are as important in the examination of witnesses as they are throughout the rest of the case.

But let me give you three rules that specifically relate to examination. They are the *never forgets* and the *never turn* Rules.

NEVER FORGET THAT THE AVERAGE WITNESS SPEAKS FROM MEMORY

Pause and consider this for a moment. We are not referring to expert witnesses here, or police officers: witnesses like this usually come equipped with notes of one kind or another. We are talking about the average, lay witness, the person who saw or heard something and now comes to tell us about it. Focus on the word 'memory' and realise what a variable, imperfect thing memory is. Consider how it usually works.

People see or hear something. They perceive it with one or more of their senses. Inevitably they interpret what they have perceived and it is this *interpretation of their perception* which they store in their *memory*.

There are two opportunities for error here: first, their interpretation may be at fault; second, their recollection will almost certainly be less than perfect. What usually happens is that witnesses to something think about it afterwards. Much of what they witnessed they remember clearly, but there are usually ragged edges to their recollection, bits where their perception was incomplete. These bits worry them. They are uncomfortable. If you are trying to remember something you want a complete picture, *an account that makes sense to you.* So you worry away at the edges, trying to make them fit comfortably with the rest of what you remember.

All this is pretty much a subconscious process, but everybody does it. It is an unusual person who can happily say, 'This much I remember. It doesn't make complete sense but that's OK by me.' Most of us keep worrying away at it, trying to make total sense of our recollection. And in so doing we rub off the rough edges. Only when we have done that, only when we have a recollection we are really comfortable with do we fix it in our memory.

But once we have shaped our recollection so that we are comfortable with it, then stored it in our memory, we tend to guard it rather jealously. Ask us to admit we were wrong and you are asking us to return to the state of discomfort we were in before we rubbed off the rough edges. Do remember that this is almost everybody's subconscious reaction. We tend to regard an attack on our memory as an attack on us personally. Our egos are involved. We can get quite stubborn in defence of what we believe we perceived and what we believe we remember. *So*

NEVER FORGET YOU ARE NOT DEALING WITH FACTS BUT WHAT THE WITNESS BELIEVES TO BE FACTS

If you bear this rule in mind and also bear in mind how stubborn most of us are in defence of our beliefs, you will remember to:

GO GENTLY WHEN YOU ATTACK A WITNESS'S RECOLLECTION

If you are gentle, if you appear genuinely reluctant to be disturbing a fixed recollection, the witness is unlikely to get stubborn. If you can sympathetically show the witness that, in one respect at least, his memory *must* be at fault, then, provided you are always gentle, he may be willing to agree that he can't really be sure about anything. If you find one little crack in his recollection, and demonstrate it to him with kindness, he is quite likely to surrender completely. I've seen it happen again and again, and in this way entire cases can just be made to fall apart. Be gentle with a witness's recollection: it has to be treated as carefully as his self-respect.

Now the 'never turn' rule:

NEVER TURN TO A WITNESS FOR HELP

This rule has a general and a specific application. Generally, it cautions you to prepare so carefully that your control is as near total as you can make it. Never make the mistake of thinking that the witness will somehow compensate for sloppy control on your part. She won't.

Specifically, what can happen is this: the lawyer has not prepared as fully as he should and he doesn't know exactly what the witness can and cannot say. A question comes from the judge or perhaps from the jury. The lawyer doesn't know the answer and he blankly and helplessly hands it over to the witness to deal with. Whatever happens at that point, he has no one but himself to blame. He has failed in his preparation. There is no adequate remedy for such a situation. Try not to get into it.

Now, a few hints of general application in the examination of witnesses, then we'll come to examination in chief, cross-examination and re-examination. This is

THE ONE LINE OF TRANSCRIPT OBJECTIVE

You have all seen a transcript, or will quite soon. One line of transcript contains between 10 and 14 words. It is a good discipline to try to make your questions occupy not more than one line. Of course there are times when you can't accomplish this. Some questions are necessarily much longer. But it's an excellent thing to aim for, and if you always keep the *One Line of Transcript* ideal in your mind your examinations will be workmanlike, easy to follow, and almost certainly more effective.

If you do aim for One Line of Transcript you probably won't need the next hint, but here it is anyway:

DO NOT ASK MULTIPLE QUESTIONS

'Were you at the junction and did you see . . .?' are two questions rolled into one. It's terribly obvious that you should ask only one question at a time, but lawyers are constantly offending against this rule and attracting quite unnecessary interventions as a result. *Next*:

ENSURE THAT YOU ASK QUESTIONS
RATHER THAN MAKE STATEMENTS

You often hear an advocate make a statement which he hopes to turn into a question by an upturn in his voice towards the end. It's unprofessional and it can look awful on the transcript. *There are four proper ways of framing a question.*

First, an actual simple question:

'Where were you on the night of June the 3rd?'

Second, a command:

'Tell her Honour and the jury where you were on the night of June the 3rd.'

Third, an invitation:

'Would you tell the jury where you were on the night of June the 3rd?'

Fourth, a declaration and request for confirmation:

'On the night of June the 3rd you were in the Campden Arms, Islington. Is that correct?'

The last of these, of course, is a leading question. Use it with care. The other three, on the other hand, should be used constantly. It is one of the surest signs of a very inexperienced advocate, examining a witness, that he only uses the first kind. He asks questions but never extends invitations and never gives commands. The result is a stilted performance that sounds unnatural. Make a point of varying the form of your question. I won't go so far as to suggest you should use question, invitation and command in mechanical rotation, but variation of form is vitally important if you want your examination to come across as real and interesting.

And as a final general hint:

BEWARE OF DEMANDING THE YES OR NO ANSWER

If you do, you risk sounding like a bully, you'll almost certainly offend against the *Don't Sound Like a Lawyer* Rule, and you may alienate both judge and jury. People know it's an interrogator's question, and they also know that the answer is almost invariably 'Yes, but . . .'. If you demand a yes or no answer and get a 'Yes, but . . .', you simply dare not brush aside the 'but'. If you do you will be seen to be unfair and you will have abandoned your role as Honest Guide. It's terribly dangerous.

But it's tempting, isn't it? The 'Answer-this-Yes-or-No' question is such a precision tool. What a shame it's too dangerous to use.

It's not. With a slight modification you can certainly use it, and in total safety. What you do is remove the atmosphere of interrogation by adding in a little kindness and courtesy and turning your demand into a request.

'Mr Witness, would you answer my next question Yes or No if you possibly can: were you in the Campden Arms, Islington on the night of June the 3rd?'

By framing the question in this way you are reasonable, you are seen to be reasonable and you are felt to be reasonable by your factfinder. You've effectively asked the witness, 'Are you capable of this?', and your factfinder knows that of course he's capable of it. If he messes you about with a 'Yes, but . . .' answer after such a fair question, he's the one who loses status, not you.

'Again, if you possibly can, yes or no to my next question: did you see Rosie O'Grady there that night?'

Don't overdo it. It's the same as all the other techniques of smooth advocacy: if you overdo them they begin to be noticeable. All techniques should be used much as you'd use spices and garlic in good cooking. They make the meal yet none of them obtrudes.

Now let's come to examination in chief, cross-examination and re-examination.

EXAMINATION IN CHIEF

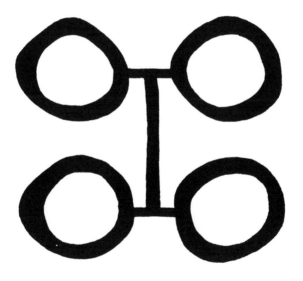

Examination in Chief

There are *two* technical rules applying to examination in chief which are so important they must be thought of as Golden. They are easily and briefly explained but they must be completely understood.

THE RULE ABOUT LEADING QUESTIONS

We've already examined the leading question and seen how it can devalue the evidence. And we've already noted that you are forbidden to use leading questions when examining your own witnesses. There are, however, at least four basic exceptions to this and you must know what they are.

Leading questions by consent. You can always use leading questions if your opponent agrees. There are usually parts of a case where little is in issue. In order to save time and charge through those areas you and your opponent may agree in advance that you can lead. Do take care, however, and, permit me to repeat myself: it may save time and make it easier for you, but don't forget if the evidence comes from you the factfinder may regard it as almost worthless. They may also feel the witness is only saying what you want her to say, and this may infect the factfinder's attitude towards the rest of her evidence – *and* towards you. Balance the advantages and disadvantages. Using leading questions by consent saves time and effort but may not be worth the cost.

Undisputed facts. Even without the consent of your opponent, these can be brought out by leading questions. You know from the pleadings or the committal papers what isn't in dispute. But the same considerations we've just discussed apply here. Don't lead if you feel the devaluation of the evidence might harm you.

Indisputable facts. Some things are so obvious and incontrovertible everybody knows them to be true. You can lead these and there is no risk involved.

Getting a denial. Here you have no choice. You have to use a leading question. 'Were you in the Campden Arms, Islington on the night of June the 3rd' – 'No.' The rules always permit you to ask a leading question so as to get your own witness to deny something.

In the United States there is another, technical, rule which *has* to be obeyed in examination in chief. Although we don't have it in England it's useful to know about because it provides you with what might be thought of as a structuring tool. Examination in chief is one of the most difficult things to do well, and this is so because so few guidelines exist on how to do it. This American, mandatory rule provides at least one guideline, and if you voluntarily follow it, your examination in chief will be tidier and more taut. It's known as the 'Foundation Rule', and it says:

> BEFORE YOU ASK QUESTIONS ON ANY TOPIC
> YOU SHOULD *LAY A FOUNDATION* SHOWING
> THAT THE WITNESS IS COMPETENT TO
> ANSWER

Think of it this way:

> A WITNESS CAN'T TELL YOU
> *WHAT* SHE KNOWS UNTIL SHE HAS TOLD YOU
> *HOW* SHE IS ABLE TO KNOW IT.

Illustration:

'Mrs Jones, you have told us you were standing on the corner of Grove Road and Nolton Street, correct?'
'Yes.'

'What colour were the traffic lights for Grove Road?'
'Objection!'
'Sustained.'

What has been left out? The witness hasn't told us she was in a position to see the traffic lights. More than that, she hasn't told us that she *did* see them. Until she tells us these things there is no 'foundation' for her to say what colour the lights were.

It's as easy as that, but if an American lawyer doesn't know the rule – and many don't – he can be well-nigh reduced to tears by the objections he will attract every one of them sustained against him. He wouldn't be able to work out what he was doing wrong; he'd have the jury looking at the ceiling or examining their fingernails and he'd probably never recover their attention.

Although it's not mandatory in England this requirement of laying a foundation runs all the way through the skilful examination of witnesses, so get into the habit of thinking properly. Try asking yourself those coupled questions: *how* did the witness perceive *what* she perceived?

How? What? How? What? If you develop this habit of rocking between How? and What? your examinations will have a rhythm to them. They'll be clearer and easier to follow.

So what other rules apply to examination in chief? At the risk of repeating myself, *all* the Golden Rules discussed so far. Every one of them. There's no need to go over them again. But there *are* two techniques I'd like to share with you.

Very occasionally your opponent will lean across just as you are about to start examining in chief, and say, 'Would you please not lead at all?' Could you do it? An advocate who can't isn't much of an advocate, and if you don't know how, it's one of the most difficult things to do.

No leading questions. The witness is sworn. 'Yes, Mr Still', says the judge.

'Mrs Snooks,' you begin, 'where were you on the night of June the
3rd 1987?'

'Really, my Lord!' says your opponent, 'My friend has just led the
witness on a date!'

You have, haven't you? You put the date into the witness's mouth.
Suppose it's a criminal case and this is an alibi witness. The date will
be of crucial importance, and you've just devalued everything the
witness may have to say. So how would you avoid this? Use a little
lateral thinking. Let me share with you a technique that always
works.

'Mrs Snooks, thank you for coming to court. Tell me if you would,
do you know why you were asked to come?'
'It's about that fight I saw, isn't it?'
'What fight was that?'
'The one in the Campden Arms, Islington.'
'Are you telling us that you saw a fight in the Campden Arms,
Islington?'
'Yes.'
'Could you tell these ladies and gentlemen the date when you saw
that fight? And for the moment could you please just answer yes or
no?'
'Yes.'
'Is there some reason why you are able to remember the date?'
'It was my wedding anniversary.'
'Very well. Would you tell us the date when you saw the fight at the
Campden Arms, Islington?'
'It was June the 3rd.'

That initial question, 'Do you know why you've been asked to come
to court?' never fails. Witnesses always know that and they are so
surprised at such an easy first question that, nervous or not, they give
you an adequate answer. And once you've got started you're away.
Notice, by the way, the *foundation* we laid before asking her to tell us
the date: how did she know it, before what that date was.

The *Murphy Method*: I've already talked about a kind of 'rocking
rhythm' you can get going by combining *How?* and *What?* questions

–first laying the foundation then bringing out the facts. If you do this, your examination in chief will move forward in *coupled* questions, and although I can't tell you why, this gives an examination a very satisfying feel.

There's another way you can introduce *coupled* questions into examination in chief. It was identified for me by my old and learned friend, Peter Murphy, the editor of *Blackstone's Criminal Practice*, and I commend it to you. It simply recommends that you organise your questions into pairs, the first of them general, and the second specific. Illustration:

'Mrs Snooks, you've told us you were in the Campden Arms, Islington on June the 3rd. Did you see anyone you recognised?'
'Yes.'
'Tell us who you saw.'
'I saw the defendant.'
'Had you ever seen the defendant before?'
'Yes.'
'When had you seen him before?'
'He'd been at the Campden the previous week.'
'And on that previous occasion did you see him do anything?'
'Yes.'
'Would you tell us what you saw him do?'

Notice that the first question always contains a very open, generalised inquiry. Did you *ever* . . .? Did you see him do *anything*? Did you see *something*? When you get the answer yes, your next question asks for specific details. If you try to think in coupled questions your direct examinations should be easy to do and elegant to listen to.

Very well. Let's come to cross-examination.

CROSS-EXAMINATION

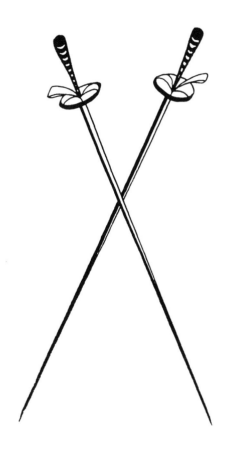

Cross-Examination

Now what special rules apply here? We have already dealt with a lot of them. If I said nothing more and you put into operation all the Golden Rules discussed so far you'd be a far better cross-examiner than most. But which of the Rules are most important for cross-examination?

THINK CONTROL

KNOW THE ANSWER YOU WANT TO HEAR AND GET THERE BY A SERIES OF QUESTIONS THAT CAN ONLY ATTRACT ONE ANSWER

THE GOODS-TRAIN APPROACH, WAGON BY WAGON, OBJECTIVE BY OBJECTIVE

BE LIKEABLE

Be Likeable is as important in cross-examination as at any other time in the case. You don't want the factfinder to start feeling sympathetic with the witness because you are giving her a hard time. If you do turn nasty as you butcher a witness, make absolutely sure that the jury feels it's justified. Eye contact is terribly important here.

THINK BEGINNING, MIDDLE AND END

Particularly think about how you are going to end. Don't just run out of things to ask. It's terrible theatre. Try to end on a high note.

There *are* special rules for cross-examination and we'll come to them. Before we do, though, let's be very clear in our minds what cross-examination is actually for. Let's take just a little time to consider some practical philosophy. What are its purposes? There are only two objectives:

First: if the evidence is damaging to your case you want to show that it is *not safe to rely on* in arriving at the final opinion.

Second: whether the witness is damaging to you or not, he may be able to give evidence which is useful to your case. If so, cross-examination is the time to get that evidence out.

Those are the two purposes. There aren't any others. The second of these – getting out extra useful evidence – needs no comment, except for the warning: 'Do it carefully'. But the first purpose of cross-examination – showing that the evidence is *unreliable* – calls for careful consideration.

Let's stand back for a moment and ask the general question: *Why* might evidence ever be unreliable? Ask the question and the answer is obvious: it comes from a *witness* who for some reason is unreliable. Our question therefore becomes: *For what reasons might a witness be unreliable?* And we can make a short list:

● The witness may not have correctly interpreted what he perceived. He may not have understood what he saw or heard. He may have jumped to a conclusion which was incorrect.
● The witness's memory may be at fault.
● The witness may be dishonest and intentionally trying to deceive the factfinder.

Putting it shortly the witness may be *wrong, forgetful or dishonest.* And of course it may be any combination of those three.

Let's consider the possibility the witness might be just wrong. Why might this be? He might not have seen clearly. He might not have heard clearly. More important, he may not have understood clearly. He might have rubbed off the rough edges of his perception and stored something completely inaccurate in his memory. What should the cross-examiner do here? Surely, you have to discover exactly what the witness *perceived* and separate this out from what he *concluded*. You have to discover how far his perception went, reduce it to the hard facts. It is your factfinder, not the witness, who is supposed to draw conclusions.

When you do reduce it to hard facts you will almost *always* find that those hard facts come in a surrounding package of uncertainty. If you explore that *Perimeter of Uncertainty* you will get a lot of *Don't Know* answers. The more *Don't Knows* you get, the less reliable the evidence feels.

But that is an incidental benefit. The only way of discovering what hard facts the witness actually remembers is by mapping out his *Perimeter of Uncertainty*.

Once you know what the witness believes his hard facts actually are, then you consider his *forgetfulness* or his *dishonesty*.

How do you explore a witness's *forgetfulness*? Again, you can use the *Perimeter of Uncertainty* approach, asking him what he remembers of the surrounding circumstances. The more 'I don't remembers' you get the more unreliable the evidence tends to seem.

But when it comes to the question of forgetfulness, the best weapon of cross-examination is what the lawyers call a *prior inconsistent statement*. In ordinary language: Has he given another, differing account on some earlier occasion? If you are lucky enough to have a prior inconsistent statement – in a deposition, or in correspondence or in a statement to police officers – then you can ask the witness about this. Show him the statement or whatever, get him to agree that his evidence in court is different from what he said on that earlier occasion. This cannot fail to undermine his present reliability.

Two warnings, however:

First: use your judgment, and don't waste time with little, unimportant inconsistencies. If you flog a point the factfinder thinks is trivial you lose all your credibility as Honest Guide and no longer appear to be fair.

Second: when you have got the witness to admit the inconsistency *do not ask him how it can be explained*. Leave that to your opponent. It's a very natural human reaction, when you've exposed an inconsistency, to say, 'Well! How do you account for that?' Don't do it. If you do the witness may give you an explanation – which may or may not be truthful – and you'll have muddied the point, perhaps even lost it altogether. It's far better, once you have exposed an inconsistency, to *leave it there* and move on to something else. You can be sure that the factfinder's human reaction will be the same as yours. They will be sitting there, silently asking 'Well! How do you account for that?' If that is how they feel they are unlikely to regard the witness as reliable.

Come now to the *dishonest witness*, and realise that dishonesty comes in different shapes and sizes. Some witnesses are blatantly dishonest, others only slightly so. Some come to court with the outright intention of lying from start to finish. Others may be almost unconsciously dishonest, telling no outright lies at all, but slanting their evidence in favour of their side. Some experts fall into this category.

So ask yourself: *Why might a witness be dishonest?*

There are only four possible reasons:

● He may have a *direct personal interest* in the outcome.
● He may have a *bias* in favour of his side.
● He may feel that the truth will not lead to a just result.
● He may be just plain malicious. This category isn't common, but the first two are.

If you feel the witness has a direct personal interest in the outcome, or a bias in favour of his side, then clearly this is something that should be explored in cross-examination. If you can show this to the factfinder they are more likely to feel that the evidence is *unreliable* – which is your objective.

Most lawyers never analyse out cross-examination like this. They learn to do it by trial and error but never focus on these underlying principles. They are so important. Have them somewhere in your mind at all times. What are the two purposes of cross-examination?

What is memory? Why might a witness be dishonest? Is it self-interest, bias or malice? Separate out what the witness perceived from what the witness concluded. Remember, all you are trying to do is to show that the evidence is less than reliable. Remember these half dozen fundamentals. Set them up like giant signposts in your advocate's mind. Keep glancing at them. Be aware they are there. If you forget these you'll start to wander, and a wandering cross-examiner is a sorry sight.

Now with this as your road-map we can look at the golden rules which apply to cross-examination. They are all short. They are all easy to understand and remember, but if you don't know them – if you break them – you and your client will probably be in deep trouble. There are 15 of them, but don't be alarmed at the number. Six of them are *Do* Rules; nine of them *Don't Ever* Rules. Let's see what they are. First, the *Do* Rules.

You've heard this one before and you must remember it:

BE AS BRIEF AS YOU CAN

There is a special reason for this in cross-examination, quite apart from your constant duty to save your factfinder's time. Almost all witnesses get more confident and more effective the longer you cross-examine them. Why is this?

When you stand up to cross-examine, the witness is almost bound to be wary of you. At this point you have an enormous advantage: *he doesn't know how much you know.* If he has been slanting his evidence, especially if he's been telling lies, he is afraid of you and of what you might have up your sleeve.

During the first five minutes he is assessing the situation, estimating how dangerous you are. It's a rare witness who starts taking liberties with you at the outset. But the longer you go on without hurting him the more confident he's going to get. The more confident he gets, the less easy he is to control.

You may be intending to lull him into a sense of confidence. It's useful to do this sometimes. But if that is *not* what you're trying to do, you should never let it happen. If you can get everything done with a witness during those first few minutes, so much the better. If you need longer, if it's one of those cross-examinations that can't be done quickly, make sure you use those first minutes to convince him that he dare not relax. All these things are encompassed by the *Be Brief* rule.

This next rule is very simple, but not always easy to put into operation:

STOP WHEN YOU GET WHAT YOU WANT

You know the answers you want to hear. You planned it meticulously in advance. You've got them. *Sit down*. The reason why it's often difficult to follow the rule is that cross-examining successfully can be enormous fun. It's like finding lift in a sailplane, playing strokes in cricket, finding your very best form at golf. You don't want to stop. Remember this danger. Don't *indulge yourself*. If you do, things may very well start to go horribly wrong. Enjoy the delights of cross-examination when they arrive, but don't clutch at them.

Next: until you get some real experience behind you it's a good idea in cross-examination to:

USE LEADING QUESTIONS

It's easier to control the witness this way. You already know what he's said on earlier occasions – in deposition or in statements to police officers. You can exercise total control over his evidence if you use the fourth kind of question we discussed earlier – *the declaration and request for confirmation*. Illustration:

'In June 1987 you were in the Campden Arms. That's right isn't it?'
'Yes.'
'You were there on the 3rd of June. Correct?'
'Yes.'
'And on the 3rd of June you were there at 9.30 in the evening weren't you?'
'Yes.'
'You had arrived, I think, at about 9.15. Is that right?'
'Yes.'

'And you arrived in the company of a young woman. Again, correct?'
'Yes.'

When you are cross-examining there is little risk that leading questions will devalue the evidence, and they do keep the witness on a tight rein. When you've got some experience, on the other hand, move cautiously in the direction of using non-leading questions as much as you can. It is always better for the evidence to come out of the witness's own mouth. The ideal cross-examination is a combination of both leading and non-leading questions.

There are two ways of expressing this next rule. Think of it under the title that appeals to you more. It's the rule that says:

PIN DOWN THE WITNESS

or, putting it another way

DON'T SPRING THE TRAP UNTIL
THE WITNESS IS INSIDE

What does this rule mean and when does it have to be followed? Remember our overall objective: showing this witness's evidence is not safe to rely on. We can do this in three ways, quite apart from showing self-interest or bias:

● We can show it is *internally inconsistent* – he's contradicting himself in the box.
● We can show it is *inconsistent with what he's already said* – he's contradicting what he said before.
● We can show it is *inconsistent with other evidence* – he's contradicting other witnesses or the evidence of documents, photographs and so on.

There's a fourth way as well: once in a blue moon you can show that a witness's evidence is plain incredible – not believable by sensible people. But that's a rarity and I'm not going to take up time on freak situations. Let's stick to what you are likely to meet: internal inconsistency, inconsistency with an earlier statement, and inconsistency with other evidence.

When you have one or more of these, then the *Pin him Down – Don't Spring the Trap too Soon Rule* must be followed. All it amounts to is this: before you face him with the inconsistency, *make absolutely certain he commits himself to the account he's now giving.* Get him to box himself in. Get him to close the door on himself. Get him to tell the factfinder that this is his evidence, no doubt about it. Get rid of all the ifs and buts. Close all the gaps he might try to slither through. Get him to commit himself, to pin himself down.

Only when you've done that do you produce the inconsistency and face him with it – if, indeed, you produce it at all. If the inconsistency arises out of his conflict with the other evidence, *you do nothing more.* Just save it up for your final speech. If the inconsistency arises because he's contradicted himself, again, *leave it there.* Save that, too, for your final speech. You have nothing to gain by facing him with it except a dramatic flourish, and even though you've boxed him in you have no guarantee he won't be able to argue his way out of his inconsistency.

You only face a witness with an inconsistency when you have proof that he said something different on an earlier occasion. And even then you do it with utmost restraint. The steps are:

First, get him to commit himself, pin himself down.

Second, get him to admit his earlier inconsistent statement.

Third, move on! Do not, repeat, do *not* give him the chance to explain. Leave it to your opponent to bring out any explanation in re-examination – if there is an explanation, and if she has the wit to remember to do it. If you do anything other than move on to something else, you are playing with fire. We'll come back to this when we consider the Don't Ever Rules.

Meanwhile, the last *Do* Rule.

Unless you are skilful and lucky you are going to hit the occasional rough patch in cross-examination. You'll get an answer that knocks you off balance, that appears to damage your case. How you handle that depends on the circumstances. No one can advise you without knowing the facts. But the Golden Rule you *must* observe is this:

RIDE THE BUMPS

Another way of saying it is:

KEEP YOUR DISMAY SECRET

Do not show by a flicker on your face that you feel you have hit a bump. Remember the Video Dimension. Don't look troubled unless you intend to. Remember the Honest Guide and the Tour Operator. What are your tourists going to think if they see you turn white or appear upset?

Quite apart from anything else, they may not have noticed the significance of the answer. If you make a big deal out of it they *will* notice. If you signal your distress you make matters ten times worse. *And* you'll be breaking the mandatory rule that says *No Opinion from the Advocate*: show them your dismay and you are broadcasting your *opinion* on the answer you got. You lose all the way down the line. In the face of a dreadful answer, *stay calm, look relaxed and move on.*

If it's an absolutely devastating answer you may like to use an old advocate's technique. In truth, it's an old advocate's *trick*, and I don't like or recommend anything that smacks of trickery. But it's very old, it's perfectly moral and it doesn't involve dishonesty of any kind. Sometimes it works quite wonderfully. It's this. When you get that pole-axing answer, *look quietly pleased.* Say to the witness:

'Give me a moment. I'd like to write that down. See if I get it right.'

Then write it down, telling him, word by word, what you are writing. Then look at him:

'Is that your evidence, Mr Snooks? Yes? Very well. Let me turn to something else for a moment.'

If you look quietly satisfied about the whole thing you deflect as much of the damage as can possibly be deflected.

Those then are the six *Do* Rules.

Come now to the *Don't Ever* Rules, and start with a rule that's very similar to the one we've just been talking about. In a way it's the same advice expressed the other way around but it's such important advice it's worth having it both ways:

THE MINEFIELD RULE

alternatively expressed as:

NEVER JUMP BACK IN ALARM!

Although your cross-examinations should seem effortless, they are often like a journey across a minefield. You are going with infinite care all the way, but suddenly your toe touches a mine. Alarm bells go off in your head. What do you do? You do *nothing that anybody notices*. Stay dead calm and act relaxed. You know you daren't go ahead but you mustn't let anyone see that you've suddenly come to an abrupt stop. Think fast about what the witness said in answer to your last few questions. Pick something out of that, anything unimportant and safe, and say:

> 'Let me go back for a moment. Did I understand you correctly? You said so and so. Is that right?'
> 'Yes.'
> 'Very well. Let me turn to . . ..'

And you are out of trouble.

This isn't tricky-lawyer game-play. This is you making certain that you don't inject your opinion into the case. If you think something's going badly wrong for you, keep quiet about it. You could be mistaken, and it's your factfinder's opinion that matters, not yours.

But let's look at some absolutely basic *Don't Ever* Rules:

DON'T CROSS-EXAMINE AT ALL
UNLESS YOU HAVE TO

It's a great way of destroying the impact of a witness just to say, 'No questions, my Lord'. You'll know what a powerful effect this has when somebody does it to you. You've gone to all the trouble of getting the witness to court, you've done your best, and your opponent brushes it all aside with, 'No questions, my Lord'. The effect on the factfinder is real.

Ask yourself: 'Has this witness done me any harm at all?' If he hasn't, think fast. Do you have anything to gain by cross-examining? You'll know your objectives from your preparation. You know what material you've got ready to show he's not safe to rely on. But do you need to use it? If he's done no harm to your case, why bother? If he has extra and useful evidence that you want to get out, think fast again. How useful will it be? Can you live without it? Weigh up the pros and cons. If you are pretty sure he's going to give you something good, then go for it. If you're less than sure give him the brush-off. Ignore him. It's great theatre if you can.

Next Golden Rule:

DON'T GO FISHING

With all the Rules you have so far you're not likely to break this one. But it's the sure sign of an incompetent. Trial is not the time for discovering information. Cross-examination is not the time for picking about and seeing what you can find. it's a time for presenting planned evidence to the factfinder. If you are stupid enough to go fishing in trial you deserve anything you catch.

The next Golden Rule is a close cousin:

DON'T ASK QUESTIONS TO WHICH
YOU DON'T KNOW THE ANSWER

Go right the way back to the woman in the short story complaining about her lawyer boyfriend/husband:

'. . . you've thought out in advance the answer you want to hear, and your question always leads you to getting that answer.'

You are working towards hearing what you want to hear, getting the witness to give you the answers you have planned in advance. With one exception, there's no room in cross-examination for asking questions when you don't know the answer you are almost guaranteed to get. And what's that exception?

You remember the *Perimeter of Uncertainty*. You are testing the witness's perception by finding out what its limits are. You might be testing her memory, her forgetfulness, by probing those limits. Here you are bound to be asking questions to which you don't know the answer. *But you aren't taking any risks.* It doesn't matter what the answers are if you plan your questions with utmost care. Probing the limits of perception and memory you are asking about things that don't really matter. They are only relevant because you are 'testing the witness's recollection' and you never expose yourself to danger.

Next rule: this should be an obvious one in light of everything we've talked about:

NEVER ASK 'WHY?' AND NEVER ASK 'HOW?'

If you do, you abandon all control: you throw the field wide open. The witness can say anything she wants to say – just about. You can't cut her off by complaining she isn't answering the question. Almost *anything* is responsive to a question that asks *How?* or *Why?* Those words are to be voided like the plague in cross-examination.

Next:

DON'T OPEN THE DOOR

Back, yet again, to our First Dimension: we are not on a search for the truth at this stage of the game. We are making a presentation to the factfinder. The rules of evidence are keeping certain things out. You want them kept out, don't you? If you do, then make absolutely sure you don't so much as hint at them in cross-examination. Don't come anywhere near them: don't breathe a word about them.

If you do, you risk *opening the door*. And what does that mean? It means that your opponent will be able to open up the whole can of worms in re-examination. The factfinder will come to hear about all kinds of things you never intended to see the light of day. And one of the Official Facts of human existence, just like the other of Murphy's various laws, is that a can of worms, once opened, cannot be re-canned in open court.

The rule *Don't Open the Door* is a very old one and goes under its very old name. I think it's time it got renamed. You may care to remember it as the Golden Rule which says:

NEVER OPEN CANS OF WORMS IN THE PRESENCE OF THE FACTFINDER

There's no excuse for it and it almost certainly loses the case for you.

That's obviously an important one. Two short ones now, and then the last of them:

DON'T LET THE WITNESS REPEAT THE EVIDENCE SHE GAVE IN CHIEF

This is because of the risk that the more your factfinder hears something the more they subconsciously embrace it as the truth. Foolish advocates often start a cross-examination by going over what the witness just said in answer to the opponent's questioning. If there's a reason for it, if, for instance, you are getting him to commit himself before springing a trap on him, then do it. But if you haven't got a good reason for it, don't do it at all. You have no excuse for rambling about in this way while you get acclimatised to being on your feet and while you wonder what you ought to be asking him.

Next:

DON'T EVER GET INTO AN ARGUMENT WITH A WITNESS

If you do, you lost your status as Honest Guide, you lose points in the eyes of your factfinder – and you may lose the argument.

Maintain your distance: remember you are a professional, doing a professional job.

Last Golden Rule, and a great one, worth saving for the end. Like *Show them the Way Home* it subsumes so many others. This is the Rule which says:

DON'T ASK THE FATAL FINAL QUESTION

Take this as an example that everybody knows:

'You've testified my client bit off the end of the victim's nose?'
'Yeah, I have.'
'And this was in the bar of the Ball and Chain. Right?'
'Yeah.'
'It's a long bar, isn't it?'
'I suppose so.'
'Forty feet, or more?'
'If you say so.'
'And it's got very dim lighting, hasn't it?'
'You could say that, yeah.'
'You were at the entrance end of the bar, weren't you?'
'Yeah.'
'And the fight took place at the other end didn't it?'
'Yeah.'
'Over 30 feet away from you, right?'
'Yeah.'
'And the bar was crowded, wasn't it?'
'Twenty or 30 people between you and the fight?'
'Yeah, about that number, I suppose.'

How's he doing, this cross-examiner? Has he shown the factfinder that this witness's evidence is less than reliable? Dreadful lighting, obscured view, considerable distance from the event. Great so far. Listen while he screws up completely.

'So how is it you say my client bit that man's nose off?'
'As he was leaving he walked right past me and I saw him spit it out!'

That's what's meant by a fatal final question. It's fatal because it loses cases. It should be called the *Foolish* Fatal Final Question, because that's what it invariably is. It's a question asked in disregard of all the other rules. It's always unnecessary and it is almost always introduced by the forbidden words How? or Why? It's a question that gets asked because the advocate *can't resist trying to end up with a flourish*, because he can't resist ending up his cross-examination with a 'There! Get out of that if you can!' And the witness gets out.

Don't do it. Don't go in for flourishes. Don't try to underline and emphasise the evidence. Don't ever give an adverse witness the chance to explain anything unless you are positive what his explanation is going to be. Never ask Why? or How? Get what you want then stop. Never ask a question to which you don't know the answer. The Fatal Final Question is always the abuse of half a dozen rules rolled into one.

Now we know exactly what we're looking at let's have another illustration. They always make great after-dinner stories, particularly if they've happened to somebody else and not you.

This one happened in a magistrates' court somewhere north of Epping. The advocate is now a respected High Court judge, which proves we can all make stupid mistakes until we've learned not to. It was in an old English market town in the dead of night. Two burglars, so the prosecutor said, were trying to break into a jeweller's shop. The police sergeant who was the main witness said in chief that he had come up to within 10 feet of the miscreants and watched what they were doing before arresting them. No one, said the defence, could have got so close without being heard. It couldn't be true. The cross-examination of the police officer was designed to show this and the defending advocate did a good job of it:

'Sergeant, would you be good enough to tell us how tall you are?'
'Six feet three inches, sir.'
'And no weakling! Would you mind telling us your weight?'
'Tip the scales at just under 20 stone, sir.'
'That night, wearing uniform were you?'
'Yes sir.'
'Helmet?'

'Yes sir.'
'Greatcoat?'
'Tunic actually, sir.'
'Boots?'
'Yes sir.'
'Regulation issue boots, sergeant?'
'Yes sir.'
'What size were they?'
'Size 12, sir.'
'Yes, I see. Size 12 boots. Studded with hobnails, were they, like the normal regulation issue?'
(Pause) 'Yes sir.'
'They had a kind of small horseshoe of metal on each heel?'
'Er, yes sir.'
'And you say you approached within 10 feet of these men without their seeming to notice your arrival, Sergeant?'
(Pause) 'Yes sir.'
'Nobody else around was there?'
'No sir.'
'Normal flagged pavements were there?'
'Yes sir.'
'I mean, you didn't approach over a lawn or grass of some kind, did you?'
(Pause) 'No Sir.'

Enough? Time to sit down? Useful cross-examination well-conducted? Get what you want then stop? One question too many coming up:

'Well, really, sergeant, can you suggest to the court how you could possibly have got as close to the defendants as you say you did without being heard?'
'On my bicycle, sir.'

Lets come to re-examination.

RE-EXAMINATION

Re-Examination

This is the most neglected corner of advocacy. Very few lawyers know what it's really for and very few do it well. So let's look at it, very briefly, and see how easy it really is.

First, what's it for? Focus on three words:

SALVAGE, CLARIFICATION AND MASSACRE

Those are its three purposes. Let's look at them separately:

SALVAGE

If your opponent knows what he's doing and has some ammunition he should be able to knock your witness about in cross-examination. You may be able to clean her up in re-examination. If you know there are satisfying reasons why she said some of the things she said – reasons which your skilful opponent avoided asking about – this is the time to bring those reasons out. In re-examination you *can* ask Why? and How? This is the first purpose. Lawyers call it *rehabilitating the witness*.

CLARIFICATION

At the end of some cross-examinations everyone is totally confused. If you leave it like that the factfinder will almost certainly treat your witness's evidence as unreliable. All they'll remember is the chaos. Your job is to tidy everything up as best you can with the quiet competence of a Mary Poppins.

'Let's go over some of what you've just been telling us, Ms Smith, and see if I'm understanding you correctly. You said . . .'

This is re-examination's second purpose – *restoring order and tidiness.*

MASSACRE

If your opponent, in cross-examination, did open a door, if he did open up a can of worms, now is the time when you gently up-end the can and spread those worms, glutinous and wriggling, all over the place. You couldn't do this before. Now, as a result of his heaven-sent incompetence, you can. Enjoy yourself. If you are careful you should be able to wipe him out. That's the third purpose – *making your opponent eat his can of worms.*

But be warned. And this warning applies to all three purposes:

IF YOU DON'T DO IT WELL IT'S
BETTER NOT TO DO IT AT ALL

If you do a weak or faltering re-examination, you play into your opponent's hands totally. You just emphasise whatever good he's done for his own case in his cross-examination.

RE-EXAMINATION MUST BE DONE
CONFIDENTLY AND EFFORTLESSLY

If you can't accomplish that, don't do it at all.

Are there any techniques to help you? There is one very important one. During cross-examination of your witness take careful written notes. Have a wide margin in your notebook, legal pad, or whatever it is you use, and as you note down what the witness is saying scribble a big letter 'R' in the margin whenever she says anything you think you might need to deal with in re-examination. This gives you at least a rough outline, and knowing the case as well as you do, this is all you'll need to guide you through.

Don't forget, incidentally, that *you are back to non-leading questions now*, but you *can* use leading questions to get out denials, and you can *also* use leading questions to refer her to things she has just said under cross-examination.

'Mrs Snooks, you said in answer to one of Mr Jones's questions that you made a statement to police officers shortly after the incident. I heard you correctly did I?'
'Yes.'
'And he asked you what you had said to them. Correct?'
'Yes.'
'He didn't ask you what condition you were in when you spoke to the police, did he?'
'No.'
'I'd like you to tell us about that now. First, how calm did you feel when you spoke to the police?'
'I wasn't calm. Somebody had to hit me across the face to stop me screaming.'

But apart from these exceptions, you must remember not to use leading questions in re-examination. Incompetent lawyers almost always forget this rule – because they've heard so many leading questions in the cross-examination they seem to catch the leading question fever – and it is disastrous for their cases to have their lame attempts at salvage and clarification pock-marked by a barrage of objections.

Done properly, re-examination can repair all kinds of cross-examination damage. Done badly it just makes everything infinitely worse. Don't do it at all unless you have to and unless you can be sure of doing it really well. Relax, stay calm, radiate quiet confidence. The Honest Guide is back in charge and about to restore sanity to the proceedings.

And when all is over and done, *don't forget the magic words*:

'Unless your Lordship has any further questions of this witness. Thank you for coming to court Ms Smith. My Lord, may this witness be allowed to leave?'

Lastly, a point which is so obvious it can easily be overlooked: your re-examination *must* be limited to things that were touched on in cross-examination. Don't ever break this rule.

And that is all I need say about re-examination. Think about it carefully. If you learn to do it well it can be a lethal sting in the tail.

FINAL SPEECH

Final Speech

Final speech, final summation, closing argument – call it what you will. This is probably the most wonderful part of the whole affair. This is where you are handed the magic wand, and where you can truly feel a linear descendant of the great orators of history.

Modern habits insist you use the language and the style of a *modern* orator, and a single Demosthenean or Ciceronian sentence would lose your listeners well before its end. But you have every opportunity the ancients had. That last speech to the factfinder is what it always was: an occasion when a speaker is given the chance to be spellbinding.

There is *no* court, and there is *no* trial where the final speech offers less than that opportunity. Those last words you say to your factfinder should always be the most persuasive and most finely judged presentation you are capable of.

Trying to tell another advocate how to do a closing speech is an intrusion. There are scraps of advice that can be thrown out, scraps sometimes so valuable they can change your whole view of the nature of advocacy. It was when I was agonising over how to argue a case that I first heard about *Show them the Way Home*. But scraps are the most one should offer. If you try to coach someone into doing a certain kind of final speech you won't help. The result will be lacking in life and, most likely, it will come across as wooden. You can't teach a person how to do a final speech. It's one of the most personal things you'll ever do as well as the most magical.

So this is a short little chapter because I'm not going to presume upon your individuality. We've shared the Rules together. You know what they are now and you've already, perhaps, begun formulating new ones for yourself. If you keep refreshing yourself on them, keep reminding yourself what they are and keep thinking about them, you'll have all the knowledge you need to produce a succession of magnificent final speeches. You know what not to do, and you'll find Newton breathing down your neck for the rest of your life. It's up to you now.

Just one *Don't*. Don't stand there and tell them everything the witnesses said. It's the biggest turn-off. Some lawyers seem to think it's their duty to start at the beginning and summarise every bit of evidence in the case. Please don't do it, or anything like it. It's insulting to the factfinder, and they sit there thinking

> 'Is this how it's done? I heard all this. Does he take me for an idiot? I suppose this is how it's done.'

It's also very boring.

But you don't need to be told this kind of thing. You would be incapable of that if you've read thus far. *You'll* be telling them yet another story. *You'll* be holding up truth after truth and inviting your factfinder to agree that this is how everything irresistibly fits together.

And emotion will be flowing.

I haven't said anything about emotion so far, but you are ready to consider it now. Emotion in advocacy is what brings everything to life. It's what charges the moment with electricity and induces the pin-drop silence.

There are rules about emotion in court – strict rules. Aristotle stated the first of them, thousands of years ago, when he was tutor to Alexander the Great:

IT'S *THEIR* EMOTION, NOT YOURS,
THAT MATTERS

He formulated other rules as well, but I don't like them. He talked, for instance, about deciding in advance precisely what emotion you want to target, and contriving a way to stir that specific feeling. Like other ancient teachers, Quintillian, for example, Aristotle strikes me as slightly cynical in his analysis. I wouldn't go so far as to castigate the ancients' analyses as dishonest, but they strike me as tricky and make me feel uncomfortable. The job we advocates are doing is an honest job, and if there is to be emotion – as there must be – then let it be honest emotion, honestly created. It *can* be done, and it is done by remembering the next rule:

EMOTION FOLLOWS FACTS
AND NOT THE OTHER WAY AROUND

I was examining the wife of a plaintiff in chief some time ago, asking her what her husband had been like before his world fell apart. She was telling us about things he used to do, how he used to behave. Then, without warning, I asked her, very simply: 'Were you lovers?'

The court, which had been quiet before, fell totally silent. There was a pause which seemed to stretch itself out endlessly. Slowly, she raised her chin and her eyes behind her glasses filled with tears.

'Yes', she whispered eventually.

In the same total silence I asked her softly: 'And how are things now?'

There was another pause. 'Different', she said, very quietly.

I sat down at that point, and my opponent didn't dare cross-examine.

There was no contrivance. It was a simple question. The facts were equally simple and they carried all their own emotion. With the greatest of respect to Aristotle, you don't need to target anything: all you have to do is give the emotion the opportunity of releasing itself.

And can we stop calling it *emotion*? That's the old, Latin, word. What we are talking about is *feelings*, and you are already familiar with the need to respect and go carefully with your factfinder's feelings. Knowing this, you have no need of another rule which says, of emotion in advocacy,

TOO LITTLE IS FATAL: TOO MUCH IS FATAL

To you, this will be obvious. And since you know about the need to keep storytelling in the forefront of your mind, you'll discover for yourself that the easiest way to reach out to your factfinder's feelings is by telling them a story. All well-told stories evoke feelings of one kind or another: it's a human response and we just can't help it.

In America the first instruction the jury is given is, 'You must not be influenced by sympathy, prejudice or passion'. In many ways this direction from the bench simply isn't realistic: of *course* the jury is going to be influenced by their feelings.

But suppose you find yourself representing the defendant in a case where your opponent really knows what she's doing. Suppose, for instance, that you were defence counsel in that case we touched on earlier in the book, on page xx, the one about the little blue car travelling across the Dales. How does one respond to the plaintiff's advocate who has told a story well and who has stirred up all kinds of feelings on the part of the jury?

It's a Golden Rule of psychology and it's equally a Golden Rule of Advocacy. We have to:

ACKNOWLEDGE THOSE FEELINGS

Agree with them. *Identify with them*. Embrace them.

Illustration

'What happened to Dr and Mrs Roe on that tragic afternoon is almost too painful to think about. You and I – all who were in court and who heard Mr Turner's opening statement – were brim-full of sympathy. It's a devastating story, and if that was the only thing we had to decide here, we could all pack up and go home. Because we are all agreed that we are involved in a tragedy.

But this is also a lawsuit and you are a jury, and we have to try to do right by everyone involved. We have to try to do justice. And doing justice, doing right, means keeping your head while admitting that your heart has been deeply affected. Let's look together at the wider picture and see what else needs to be considered by a group of fair-minded people who are bound by their oath to do right according to the law.

You will be told by the learned judge that you must not be influenced by sympathy, prejudice or passion. But of course you'll be influenced, struggle as you may. We are all influenced.

But with our heads as well as our hearts let's take a closer, careful, look at what really happened . . .'

Before I end let me just say a word about *energy*. Will you think yourself back into a time in your life when you were really at your most energetic? It's a curious little exercise that hardly takes more than a few seconds to do.

When you've identified that episode in your life, put it at the top end of the scale and now do the opposite. Think back to a time when you were at your idlest, your most utterly down and your most unproductive. And put that at the bottom end.

Now, without thinking about it, you know, don't you, almost exactly where you are on the scale at this present moment? Without any gradations of degrees or centimetres, you *know* where your energy is this instant. It's a kind of invisible yardstick you just used.

When you are before a jury, remember that yardstick is in there with you. Every juror has his or her own yardstick, and so does the judge. Your job is to keep them in the upper half of the scale. Energy levels can be read. You can see it in their eyes and you can feel it in the air. Keep their energy levels up: all feelings depend for their quality on the energy level of the individual listener. Aim to keep your factfinders at an exhilarating level, so that at the end of a court day they can't wait for the next episode. It's not impossible. It's not even difficult. Just be aware of that invisible yardstick, be nice, and keep in mind from start to finish that, if there is an element of storytelling in everything you do, you're doing it right.

Enough, then, and over to you. If you truly resolve to be one of the *real* advocates of your time, that is almost certainly what you will become. If you do as I suggested at the beginning of this book, and find 10 minutes every day to read a little and think a little about advocacy, then, shameful though it is to realise it, you will be doing much more than most of your competitors.

We've looked together at a little over 80 Golden Rules, 80 potential traps which you might have fallen into. You're not likely to do that now, but I'll tell you what you *are* going to do.

From now on, when you go into court, you are going to be infinitely more aware of how your contemporaries are performing. You are going to watch, probably with fascination, the extent to which these rules are broken – in every court and on every day when the courts are sitting. And you are going to *know* exactly what is being done wrong. You'll also know what is being done right, and you'll recognise really good advocacy as soon as you see it.

As I said quite early on, simply by being aware of these sensible Rules, you'll improve as an advocate. More than that, you'll improve rapidly. The secret is those two or three minutes every day – you don't need more – of glancing at the rules, followed up with seven or eight minutes, some time during the next 24 hours, of musing about advocacy. Do this and there's no doubt at all that you will turn into one of the better advocates. Your self-confidence will grow quickly because you'll see the results, and the more acutely you are aware of the rules the more you will find yourself putting them into effect. You will become an Honest Guide, a skilful, persuasive advocate – and you are sorely needed.

You are needed because the world we live in is moving into history's most critical phase, and, faced with the pressure of these dangerous and difficult times, the leaders of humankind are going to be more and more tempted to sidestep and override the rule of law. It always happens when the going gets tough, and the going is already getting tough.

If liberty, justice and the rule of law are to be saved and upheld, it is you and others like you who must save and uphold them. We are arriving at a time in human affairs when the truth is going to come into conflict with doublespeak and dogma as it never has before, and the role of the honest and courageous advocate is going to be a vitally important one.

More, even, than that, we are now inhabiting a world that is interconnected to a degree undreamed of in other times. There is a wild, democratic impulse sweeping the planet and, thanks to our satellites, screens and fax machines, everyone can watch and take sides as people everywhere struggle to tame the unruly beast we call democracy. There has never before been such a need, nor such an opportunity, for enlightened, skilful advocates to argue and explain and persuade.

Advocacy, honest advocacy, is about making people see the truth with a new awareness. It is about persuading people to follow this course rather than that one. All you have to do, today, is look around and you see the need for enlightenment, the need for new and different priorities, the need for completely new attitudes and actions. They *must* come. The question is: Will they be brought about by force or by persuasion? Force has had a long and bloody innings, and we are all too dangerously beweaponed to place too much faith in force.

That leaves persuasion. It could be, as we approach the millenium, that we are entering the Age of the Honest Advocate.

As I say, you are needed.